WRITERS *of* WALES

Duncan Bush

Editors:

Jane Aaron
M. Wynn Thomas
Andrew Webb

Other titles in the Writers of Wales series:

Jane Williams (Ysgafell) (2020) Gwyneth Tyson Roberts
Hester Lynch Thrale Piozzi (2020), Michael John Franklin
Emyr Humphreys (2018) M. Wynn Thomas
Christopher Meredith (2018), Diana Wallace
B. L. Coombes (2017), Bill Jones and Chris Williams
Owen Rhoscomyl (2016), John S. Ellis
Dylan Thomas (2014), Walford Davies
Gwenlyn Parry (2013), Roger Owen
Welsh Periodicals in English (2013), Malcolm Ballin
Ruth Bidgood (2012), Matthew Jarvis
Dorothy Edwards (2011), Claire Flay
Kate Roberts (2011), Katie Gramich
Geoffrey of Monmouth (2010), Karen Jankulak
Herbert Williams (2010), Phil Carradice
Rhys Davies (2009), Huw Osborne
R. S. Thomas (2006), Tony Brown
Ben Bowen (2003), T. Robin Chapman
James Kitchener Davies (2002), M. Wynn Thomas

WRITERS *of* WALES

Duncan Bush

ROBERT MINHINNICK

University of Wales Press
2026

www.uwp.co.uk

British Library Cataloguing-in-Publication Data
A catalogue record for this book is available from the British Library.

ISBN: 978-1-83772-387-4
eISBN: 978-1-83772-388-1

The University of Wales Press wishes to acknowledge the assistance of the Books Council of Wales in publication of this title.

For GPSR enquiries please contact: Easy Access System Europe Oü, 16879218, Mustamäe tee 50, 10621, Tallinn, Estonia. *gpsr.requests@easproject.com*

Typeset by Marie Doherty
Printed and bound by CPI Group (UK) Ltd, Croydon, CR0 4YY

Contents

Acknowledgements

I am grateful for the help of several editors, publishers, writers and academics who have assisted with this volume.

These include Professor Merryn Hutchings; the editors of *Wales Arts Review* for a section of *The Genre of Silence*; Assistant Professor Zoe Brigley, editor of *Poetry Wales*, for publishing three previously unpublished poems by Duncan Bush and a section of chapter 14, 'Unpublished and uncollected poems'; Dr Laura Wainwright; Paul (P.C.) Evans at the *Amsterdam Review*; Phil Cope for help with Duncan Bush's work with Valley and Vale Community Arts; the charity Sustainable Wales/Cymru Gynaliadwy for invaluable office assistance; Professor Ian Gregson, for personal communication; Mick Felton and Sarah Johnson at Seren Books; and especially Annette Weaver, for her assistance with dates, employment details and photographs, and for her permission to quote from Duncan Bush's unpublished writings.

1

Introduction

This book about the Welsh writer Duncan Bush is organised chronologically, mirroring the dates of his publications. My access to Duncan's unpublished texts,[1] offered generously by his wife, Annette Weaver, has been of great importance. A substantial amount of these texts, and of uncollected work, is used throughout, but generally discussed towards the end of the book. I hope that these will one day find full publication.

Bush was always a writer who believed in mixing his genres; thus, he can be considered a poet, novelist, short-story writer, translator, playwright, essayist, documentary-writer, reviewer and critic. Compiling this volume has given me new insights into Duncan Bush's writings.

Duncan Bush's published biographical notes in his early publications give the bare bones of his life, here partly revealed in chapter 2, 'Biography'. Yet Duncan always knew, like many new writers, that such notes, and the identities they suggested, might be experiments in fiction. As well as fluidity of literary form, he experimented with literary identity, creating at least three other personae for himself via noms de plume. These fictional people, 'poet' Pierre de La Prée and 'poet and essayist' Jay McGill, had their own biographies, published in the first issue of the *Amsterdam Review* (2004). Victor Bal, the Bush-created poet from *The Genre of Silence* (1988), also has his own scrupulously created fantasy-bio, 'A Brief Life'.

Ultimately, Duncan continued and continues to be published. His poetry features in several anthologies, such as the Library of Wales collection *Poetry, 1900–2000* (Stephens, 2007). In 2023, three of his previously uncollected and unseen poems appeared in *Poetry Wales* and were performed by others for the first time at a special event on 23 November.

In his enormous volume *Letters from Wales* (2023), Sam Adams reprints his essay originally published in *PN Review*, which lauds Bush as not only a poet but a writer of 'extraordinary fiction' (1998).

Note

1 Some of the unpublished material does not have titles: this is simply referred to as 'unpublished'. Where titles are provided they have been used.

2

Biography

Duncan Bush was born in Cardiff on 8 April, 1946. His father was Donald, a builder, as testified by a number of poems, and his mother was Linda, who at one point worked in a laundry, but who doesn't appear in any of her son's surviving poems. She died when Duncan was seventeen. However, both Donald and Linda are featured in Bush's unpublished writings, some of which have been revealed to me by Annette Weaver.

Donald Bush built the bungalow where Duncan, his older brother Allan, and their parents lived in Whitchurch, in Cardiff, and then, after Linda's death, a house outside Peterston-super-Ely, five miles west of Cardiff. Donald lived here until shortly before his death.

In his unpublished and undated papers, Bush writes both critically and in praise of Donald:

> Even now, where a new estate of housing is laid out – some unutterably drab or pretentious future suburb – I still sense what it is to be a builder of houses, a breaker of new ground, a raiser of walls.
>
> By the age of nine or ten, I was to view my father's work less romantically, via the children in the books I was reading. They had fathers who left each morning for The Office – though this, it was somehow implied, was more a sinecure than a job, and what these fictional fathers did there was mysterious. I suppose now that they were in 'The City' – that mythical hyperEnglish institution, shadowy as the Sumerian Underworld. Not, at any rate, in the factory, down the pit – or as mine was – 'on the buildings'.
>
> I clearly remember wondering with an infant's sense of grievance why we didn't have a big house and servants, like children in the children's books

> of those days. No-one else I knew in school did either, but I wasn't making comparison with my peers.

In these papers, Bush can be irritated by his father's repetition of stories. Yet, he writes:

> I regret not actually having made recordings of them in the years when my father was still in full vigour and his stories fresh, if not to me, then at least to my children who listened to him with the round-eyed fascination of the young. He liked best to talk autobiographically of his trips as a young seaman to Durban, Buenos Aires or Goa in the early 1930s, or his experience in the East End during the blitz, when he was part of a squad engaged in repairing bomb damage, but the bedrock of his life story was forty years as a bricklayer and house builder in Cardiff, a man of natural and untutored intelligence and a master craftsman in a trade frequented in those days by a Dickensian range of colourful characters, rough diamonds and desperadoes.

And he adds:

> He combined in his life and in these stories the two essential strands out of which Walter Benjamin says all literature is born: that of the sailor, who returns to the place of his birth to tell of a wider world, and the farmer, who goes nowhere but relates what happens on his native soil.
>
> Given this, I suppose I must have learnt story-telling at his knee, as well as how to read. My instinct, however, was always that of more secretive, perhaps more watchful souls; say little, but write it down later.

Allan Bush, Duncan's brother, is a retired building surveyor who has lived and worked in Cardiff all his life. He published his first novel, entitled *Last Bird Singing*, in 2008. He too might have learned 'story-telling' at his father's knee. However, until his novel was published, I was only aware of his poem 'In Memory of Benjamin Moloise (Hanged 17th October 1985)', which appeared in *Poets Against Apartheid / Beirdd yn Erbyn Apartheid* (Elfyn and Jenkins, 1986), from the Wales Anti-Apartheid Movement. Duncan Bush made two contributions to this volume.

Annette Weaver writes about the brothers (pers. corr. 2023):

> I don't think I have anything very illuminating to say about Duncan's relationship with Allan from a literary/biographical perspective. In fact they always got on quite well when they met, and we saw quite a lot of Allan and his family when we lived in Wales, but there were later frictions that, given the generally combative – and largely masculine in later years – nature of the family dynamic, went unresolved. It was unclear what caused the coolness of their relationship, and I know Duncan regretted it, but given their personalities nobody made the first move towards a thaw.
>
> I'm now in touch with Allan and his son Stephen, and all is very friendly. So it can be done.

For more on *Last Bird Singing*, by Allan Bush, see chapter 8 in this volume.

On an undated page of unpublished typescript (numbered 38, although these pages were not necessarily numbered by himself), titled 'A Sense of Place', Duncan Bush has written:

> Born in rented rooms, I spent most of the thirty-odd years of my life domiciled at dozens of other addresses (in various parts of England and Wales, and in a number of other countries), all of which – apart from the years when I lived at home in Lon y Celyn (Cardiff) – were rented too. When, later in our lives, I and my wife had enough savings to 'buy' a house to live in, what this actually meant was putting a deposit on a large mortgage, a debt which would have to be repaid at interest over decades.

Of Lon y Celyn, Bush has written (undated):

> The private housing along the stony lane of our stretch . . . was newer and stood higher on the social scale – part of the huge acreage of speculative building that was going up at the fringe of towns and cities in the 1950s. Built by small firms on plots just large enough for one or two houses, they were mostly bungalows or semis erected in pairs of varying sizes, styles and types. All seem united now in the architectural banality of the day, though there were those tiny differences – the shape of a porch or window, a 'feature' of brick arches or sills – which constituted in the minds

> of each mortgage holder a visible distinction between any one pair and its neighbours.

And he continues, in 'A Sense of Place':

> Perhaps this is one reason why I've never had much sense of belonging in or to a specific single locality. I've never even been sure whether 'belonging' in this context involves my belonging to a place or the place – a house, an area of land, ultimately an entire national territory – belonging to me. Both ideas, in any case, are illusory.

Sense of belonging, or not, is a theme which runs through Bush's writing, and is the focus of chapter 6 in this book.

Bush learned to read at an early age; Annette Weaver (pers. corr. 2023), writes: 'Duncan's mother always maintained that he could read the newspaper at the age of two.' As he wrote in an autobiographical piece 'Lash LaRue and the River of Adventure' in *Midway*: 'Reading was space travel: the imaginative extension of the self. And by the age of seven or eight I'd discovered my universe of choice lay there' (1997a).

Annette Weaver continues:

> His delight in words and in extending his vocabulary was evident throughout his school career; as a small child he enjoyed writing stories and inventing rhymes (an example from around the age of seven: pop into Asti's for a tasty pasty and make it hasty or I'll get nasty) and by the time he entered Whitchurch Grammar School it was clear that English would be his favourite subject.

Duncan Bush was commissioned to review a new dictionary in *Poetry Wales*; in his essay, 'Abecedarian to Shagtastic', he wrote:

> An unruly schoolboy, yet pedantic, even at that age, I skipped homework and mitched off classes but privately studied the dictionary on an almost daily basis, collecting new words on a principle, already clear to me, that they'd be useful – that one day I'd use them. (And now I have . . .) (2003a)

And those 'new words'? 'Abecedarian; Gleet; Transude.' I can recall, as editor, Bush accepting the commission with delighted alacrity. Bush, in his unpublished papers, writes of inheriting a family dictionary from 'Uncle Johnny':

> I still have the book, a scarlet Cassell's hardback, the spine tattered from hard use and the lists of words pencilled in the endpapers: fulvous, adscititious, internecine . . . It's clear, that for most of my early life and well into my adulthood language was an opportunity of displaying cleverness in public. (But what's writing itself except a way of showing off with words?)

The Bushes were also avid consumers of film, and more will follow on Duncan Bush and the cinema. Explicitly, his poem 'Going to the Pictures in the Fifties' revels in the whole experience, from big pictures, supporting films, the theatrical darkness, the usherettes and the ice cream, to the other late-coming adherents ('infuriating silhouettes') in those lost Cardiff auditoriums, even when pushing past his knees and scrambling over handbags:

> We craned not to miss
> even the pre-titles
> . . .
> Reality ran at twenty-four frames
> a second, and hung in dreams
> at one end of a room
> . . .
> We were looking for America, we even felt American
>
> (1997a)

– as both characters in *Sailing to America* seem to do (1997b; see chapter 7).

Bush's determined love of cinema saturates his writing. But this wasn't an easy relationship. Duncan, and the rest of his family at this time in Cardiff's north Llandaff and Whitchurch, detested the British class system, which they felt was reinforced by films of the post-war period. This is made clear in 'Lash LaRue and the River of

Adventure' (see chapter 9). It seems British culture was made ridiculous for the Bush family by the hackneyed class stereotypes those films regurgitated. The implication is that this was a world that in Britain, first skiffle music, then rock and roll, then Beatlemania helped destroy.

This childhood awareness of class divisions is also apparent in his account of trips to the seaside at Lavernock, in an unpublished and undated account with that title. He writes about public transport in the 'pre-Beeching' era, when a wide variety of local trains were still available, and before the Bush family owned its own transport. Duncan notes that private transport made other beaches, such as Llantwit Major and Ogmore-by-Sea available, but he believed such places 'had a genteel air':

> I missed the plebeian populousness, or intimacy, or coarseness, or whatever it was, of Lavernock, where I'd always found something interesting to watch or take part in. At Lavernock I never had it on my mind that I had no-one but my parents to play one-end cricket or dig out moats . . .
>
> What's certain, however, is that those born after the Fifties will never realize how important 'going down the beach' was in the city's life: part of a simultaneously marine and urban culture that I didn't meet again until I read Camus' novel L'Etranger and his essays on the Oran of his own adolescence, and the Algerian coastal landscape.

And the unpublished 'Lavernock' continues:

> What made the place, and that period, so important in my memory was the fact of having lived away for so long. But what Lavernock symbolized for me wasn't so much homesickness itself as a sort of demotic nostalgia (to use an adjective I prefer to 'working-class'.) It's difficult to define what I mean, since the terminology of class has been vitiated irrecoverably, corrupted by bias from all sides. But if the snobs yearn for some lost aristocratic Arcadia and socialists a proletarian paradise-to-be, any wistfulness I have for Lavernock is simply about personal memory, my part in a form of collective leisure: a way I and other Cardiffians had of spending summer Sundays in the open air in the 1950s.

Annette Weaver's letter (pers. corr. 2023) adds that:

> Duncan was . . . a talented artist, possibly an inheritance from his signwriting grandfather, and decided to take Art along with History and English at A level. At the same time he was a keen footballer, playing in goal for the school team, as well as pursuing a lifelong interest in cricket.

These sporting interests are reflected in some of his later writing. Annette Weaver continues:

> But he became disillusioned with education. Following the death of his mother when he was seventeen – an event that came as a profound shock, as he had been kept in ignorance of the seriousness of her illness— on leaving school he was disinclined to follow the nowadays expected next step of university. Nobody in his immediate family had ever done such a thing, and instead he went out to work, firstly for his father in the building trade, then a stint in an office in London, as well as various temporary jobs.

She adds:

> In his early twenties he decided to try Swansea University but left after a year and went back to working as a pipefitter and crane driver among other things, although he remained living in Swansea.

Bush I believe successfully uses his experiences gleaned from such employment in his writings, especially in earlier poems such as 'Drainlayer', some later ones like 'Gill', and in his second novel, *Glass Shot*. But in his late twenties Duncan Bush entered Warwick University as a mature student, studying English and European Literature. It was at Warwick that he met his future wife, Annette Weaver, in 1975. She was pursuing an MA in Comparative Literature. Duncan's first words to Annette, she assures me, were '"What did you think of the seminar on Structuralism?" which suggested he wanted to make an impression'.

His four years at Warwick, including a scholarship to Duke University in North Carolina, ended in the best First Class degree of his year, and enabled him to go on to study for a DPhil at Wadham College, Oxford. Annette writes:

> His subject was initially based on the poetry of Swinburne; however the longer he worked on it the more he realised that his own work was his real interest, and although he remained a registered student (as far as I know) for the rest of his life, he never completed a thesis.

Duncan Bush and Annette Weaver were married on 4 April 1981 in Gravesend, and they had two sons together, Joseph (Joe), born 3 June 1981, and Lucas, born 29 August 1985. Annette comments:

> Throughout his life Duncan would go back to childhood memories, as many of us do, for connections to and reflections on present situations. He valued the state of childhood and its perceptions enormously; his own children were a constant source of delight and education to him.

Duncan worked with Annette at Thurrock College in Essex as a part-time teacher of English as a Foreign Language between 1978 and 1981. Subsequently, they both obtained positions at Atlantic College, near Llantwit Major, in Wales, where Duncan worked part-time from 1983 to 1984. From 1985, he worked as the part-time director of the Creative Writing programme at Newport College of Art, now the University of Wales Newport.

In 1995, the family moved to Luxembourg, where Annette taught at the European School. For the next ten years Duncan taught and read on various creative writing courses in Luxembourg, Germany and the UK, including Tŷ Newydd in Gwynedd, the National Writing Centre of Wales/Canolfan Ysgrifennu Cymru. From 2006 to 2014, he worked as a part-time teacher of English at the European School, Luxembourg, where Annette already worked.

Of their home in Ynyswen, south Powys, Annette Weaver writes:

> We bought the house [their first] in 1984 during the miners' strike. Duncan commuted from there to Newport from 1990 to 1995; then after we had moved to Luxembourg, he arranged his teaching in blocks so he could be in the UK for a period each term.

Duncan Bush carried on writing and tutoring until his death, from bowel cancer, on 18 August, 2017. Writing was always what he thought of as his 'real', indeed only, career.

Of her husband's death, Annette Weaver writes:

> Duncan left behind a very large amount of material: several unfinished novels, short stories, translations, articles and of course poems. Deciding what to do with this archive is a daunting task, and so far I have only done a little editing of the unpublished poems.[1]
>
> We would frequently discuss his work in progress so I feel this is a 'permitted' extension of previous (minor) contributions. What, if anything, happens to the rest remains to be seen.

This brief outline of Duncan Bush's life has introduced many of the themes that are evident in his writing, and will be discussed throughout this book. He repeatedly drew on his knowledge of and interest in tools and physical work, of film and photography, and of sport. His sense of class, and of national and international identity permeate his writing. The next chapter explores his earliest publications.

Note

1 This includes proof-reading three previously unseen pieces published in *Poetry Wales* (Bush, 2023).

3

Early publications

Three Young Anglo-Welsh Poets (1974), *Green Horse* (1978), *Nostos* (1980), *Aquarium* (1984), *Salt* (1986)

I first came across the name Duncan Bush in 1972 after reading about the poetry competition that was to result, in 1974, in the publication of *Three Young Anglo-Welsh Poets*, to which Bush contributed ten poems. He shared this volume with Tony Curtis and Nigel Jenkins. Some of these ten would also appear later in *Aquarium* and *Salt*. Yet I think it was the publication of *Green Horse: An Anthology by Young Poets from Wales* (Stephens and Finch, 1978), that drew my closer attention to Bush. He had contributed three poems to this anthology of younger writers of 'Anglo-Welsh' poetry. I attended the launch of this volume in June, 1978 in what was the Oriel bookshop in Charles Street, Cardiff. I note several contributors signed my copy, but not Bush. Thus I don't believe he was present. In fact, I don't think I met Duncan Bush until two years later.

Concerning *Green Horse*, Roland Mathias ended his foreword: '*Green Horse* offers considerable hope for the future; though whether that future will long contain what could meaningfully be called "Anglo-Welsh" poetry must be open to doubt' (Stephens and Finch, 1978). Fifty years later, the term 'Anglo-Welsh' has almost vanished and is often derided. But Welsh people persist in writing in English.

I first met Duncan Bush in Swansea, at an event to launch his third publication, the pamphlet *Nostos*, which appeared in August, 1980.

Nostos consists of twenty-four pages, published by Swansea Poetry Workshop. *Nostos* is a Greek word suggesting the return home of a hero, probably from warfare; the most famous example of this is Homer's *Odyssey*. I recall Duncan autographing my copy. One of the reviews alluded to 'giant-sized postcards' from sunnier climes (Jenkins, 1981). The critic was Mike Jenkins, poet and short-story writer, referring in *Poetry Wales* to Bush's south of France beach scenes, which were a subject for much of his writing life. Too easy a dismissal. For me, such poems were fresh and challenging. Some of the poems in *Nostos* appeared in new versions in his first collection, *Aquarium*, and such 'postcard poems' continued to be published throughout Bush's life, as in 'Postcards from Zakinthos' (*Masks*).

Following *Nostos* were *Aquarium* (1984) and *Salt* (1986), both from Seren Books, which had emerged from Poetry Wales Press. These displayed both international and personal concerns.

A feature of Bush's work which is evident in these early publications is his use of personae. Critic Christine Pagnoulle has written online (1995):

> As Richard Poole has pointed out, even in some fairly early poems such as 'Pneumoconiosis' Bush adopted the technique of writing through personae, a convenient way of widening his field of enquiry while conveying a sense of immediate experience without raising the suspicion of personal outpourings.

'Pneumoconiosis' appeared in *Poetry Wales* (Bush, 1973), but was first collected in *Black Faces, Red Mouths* (1985), and also appeared in *Salt* (1986):

> I saw my own brother: rising,
> dying in panic, gasping
> worse than a hooked
> carp drowning in air.
> Every breath was his last
> until the last.
> . . .
> Know me by my slow step,

the occasional little cough, involuntary
and delicate as a consumptive's,

and my lung full of budgerigars.

This might be one of the poems that Ian Gregson (2005) considered as linking Bush to older 'Anglo-Welsh' writing (see chapter 5). Bush wrote, creating a persona of a dying miner:

I'll die with this now.
It's in me
Like my blue scars.

The same issue of *Poetry Wales* contains Graham Allen's 'Old Colliers':

Dust, their lungs' rasped weather, dust on me.

(1973)

A very familiar theme for Welsh poets in 1973, when this edition of the magazine was published. Yet Allen, unlike Bush, does not create a persona. For myself, looking back to 1973, I see Bush's miner now linked to the personae created by Bush in his first two novels.

Terry Eagleton's quoted endorsement on the cover of *Aquarium* states that 'Duncan Bush's poetry undermines the myth that political poems are one thing, personal ones another' (Eagleton, 1984). And no poem in the volume reflects this more clearly than 'At the News of Proposed Pit Closures', where the writer combines news of his new home, 'a small house in Kent', with a listing of threatened mines, those 'shabby vineyards of industrialism' (Bush, 1984; 'shabby' rewritten from 'run-down' in the poem's original publication in *Black Faces, Red Mouths*, 1985).

Bush writes about his home country, and the tone is apt for his 'On Wales', which is 'for R. S. Thomas' (1984). Yet this dedication gives the poem an unnecessary burden. In 'Nausea' Bush reveals his R.S.-like disgust at tourists, but this time from inside a motor vehicle. R.S.-ish imagery abounds, but also:

a morose,
solitary child, too old for his parents
. . .
on the back seat.

(1984)

That, at least, is typical Duncan Bush. The solitary child is Bush himself, learning to observe – and not being satisfied with everything he sees.

There are the usual poems from first collections, such as young male writers coming to terms, or not, with alcohol. Thus, 'Saloon Bar Drinker' and 'Old Man in Scrumpy House' from *Aquarium* begin a theme that will be continued into his final collection, *The Flying Trapeze* (2012), with 'Cider Orchard Story'.

There is also this tribute, 'A Sense of the Passing, Thomas Hardy 1840–1928':

as if already
he saw
life as an old photograph of then

(1984)

which ends with what became typical Bush images of photography and 'the inappreciable / instant it took / light to reach his eyes'. For me, this is a young man's poem with its first line 'Poor Hardy, haunting his own future'. This poem is the first in a series of tributes to older 'great' writers, which will conclude in *The Flying Trapeze* (for the later tributes, see chapter 14).

In *Aquarium*, I have always noted the curious unease its author displays in 'Soleil de Miel' (originally titled 'Sur la Plage') as he sunbathes, his mood stunned by the heat in the south of France. Yet, he is almost anxious:

we're clenching fistfuls
of loose sand;

they pour the faster
the tighter we grip.

(1984)

Bush is 'dulled with wine, amnesic'. Yet at least the poet in him remains alert. Later, in 'Aquarium du Trocadero', some fish are somnolent, whilst others 'amnesic . . . stupefied . . . doped' (1984). This poem has been regularly anthologised.

Despite (or because of) the descriptions of the lithe, almost naked bodies in some of these poems, Bush is conscious that time is passing, whether we use it or not. This is a poet who in the same collection writes, in surprising lines that demand to be reread, about his firstborn son, whose 'mauve feet' are 'tender as a glans-skin', and who is 'still clumsy as a tortoise'. The new father adds:

And the future's blank, the future's always
blank –
though that
says something for it.

(1984)

Significant for the future in *Aquarium* is 'Vanishing Point 3000', with its early line 'The sky's a remote screen' (1984).

In *Salt* (1986), the poem 'The Hook' stands out for me, and I applaud the decision to make this the title of the combined selection from the first three volumes (1997). Again, a theme of work, as depicted by 'implement, not emblem', a scythe its owner calls 'the hook'. Historically and symbolically important, the poet mourns the fate bestowed on scythes:

  but mass
produced now for a dwindling few, this tool,
this weapon
. . .

> and that is beautiful only
> now; for the coarse use that refined it,
> like the sea-stone.
>
> (1986c)

Thus a 'scythe' becomes a 'hook', which illustrates the poet's fascination as to how implements are named. 'Cold-Chisel', also from *Salt*, is similar, as the poet identifies as best he can exactly what the tool is:

> Cold-
> chisel; bar; hexagon
> of steel.
>
> (1986c)

And equally important is the satisfaction that physical work with the hook, the scythe, actually brings:

> Doubled I stooped, climbing the field
> all the hot afternoon
>
> for these red stigmata,
> skinned blisters on the mounts of
> both white palms.
>
> (1986c)

The poet is enjoying his own labours here, but is always, for me, aware of his father's building career. For Duncan the scythe, for Donald, the measuring tape.

'Navvies' is one of the poet's clearest expressions of his fascination with photography, and equally its subjects. Bush introduces the poem, one of his most substantial early pieces, with a long quotation (surely used ironically) from Briggs and Jordan's *Economic History of England*: '"The north of England" . . . was flooded with hordes of half-starved, half-naked Irish, spreading diseases wherever they went. However, the Scots were by nature frugal, provident and independent' (1986c). And the actual poem has:

these women
plain, crude-featured, without
elegance, the dignification & parasol
of the studio posture, but thickened
by the labour
of work & birth,
work &,
birth,
in clumsy skirts, faces
expressing the strength of sunlight
above them
in a scowl, the lines of a frown
almost as if it were anguish

Bush's humanitarian politics is clear to everyone here. But such politics had never room for 'nationalism'. And quickly it becomes anger:

as if they were jungle-
or prairie-indians, these
nomads, living & breeding in their litter
of shacks, illness & trampled mud
at the edge
of the road or rail or water-way they are
building and following, like gypsies

Make no mistake, Bush sympathised with everyone here, including 'gypsies'. But the writer is equally interested in the mechanics of the photographic act itself:

The plate is the ancient colour
of soot
seen in sunlight.
. . .
Taken one
afternoon of now
unknowable
light in the second
half of the last

century; it is
the camera which unites
them for this
awkward
  class-photograph
they make

Bush is adamant he must pick out the photographer in the poem here. He or she is a 'documentarist and no doubt something of the sociological voyeur' (1986c).

This interest in the photographer's gaze is a recurring theme in Bush's work. Susan Sontag similarly commented:

> Even if incompatible with intervention in a physical sense, using a camera is still a form of participation. Although the camera is an observation station, the act of photographing is more than passive observing. Like sexual voyeurism, it is a way of at least tacitly, often explicitly, encouraging whatever is going on to keep on happening. To take a picture is to have an interest in things as they are, in the status quo remaining unchanged (at least for as long as it takes to take a 'good' picture), to be in complicity with whatever makes a subject interesting, worth photographing – including, when that is the interest, another person's pain or misfortune. (1979)

Part 1 of 'Navvies' is Bush's earliest example of his fascination with work and workers, always remembering that Part 2 shows the theme expanded historically into the past, whilst 'Movietone' (also in *Aquarium*) and 'Living in Real Times' (*Masks*) bring it uncomfortably into the present.

In a way this concern with photography is shared by his contemporaries, recalling that Tony Curtis's *Album* (his first significant collection of poems) appeared in 1974. But of course an 'album' might also denote popular music, especially after the mid-1960s, when albums such as Bob Dylan's *Blonde on Blonde* (1966) and the Beatles' *Sgt. Pepper's Lonely Hearts Club Band* (1967) were released.

'The lyrical treatment of manual labour' noted by Sam Adams in his 'Letters from Wales' column in *PN Review* (1998), and subsequently in his own collection of these letters (2023), is applied to 'Drainlayer' from *Salt*. Adams admires the poem's 'full rhymes, muted by enjambment, glimmering like pale stone in freshly turned dark soil' (2023).

> The blade
> cuts clean, and brightens;
> glazes earth
> the downthrust frees, the spade
>
> flings. But I bury my own
> work dark. Nothing stands
> but me:
> I lay veins, straight bone
>
> In earth for earth my daughter.
> My hollow son is
> earth too,
> exoskeleton of water.
>
> (1986c)

Bush's fascination with physical/manual work is similar to that of Nigel Jenkins. Duncan is not represented in *Common Ground: Poets in a Welsh Landscape* (Butler, 1985), but Jenkins's poem 'The Ridger' is fittingly quoted in the book's foreword:

> To describe is to listen, to enter
> Into detail with this ground
> And this ground's labour; to take
> And offer outward continuing fruit.

And

> Less patent is the deeper tale
> That gathers with the touch of rain
> On the spike which was a handle;
> The nail bent over for an axle-pin.

Bush and Jenkins are linked here by a common theme.

Symbolic in *Aquarium* are the first concerns as to what's suddenly happening to UK industry, with 'At the News of Proposed Pit Closures' and 'To the Memory of Robert Watson, Killed During the Lorry Drivers' Strike of 1979'. A little later, the miners' strike of 1984/5 would prove to be one of the most significant UK events for Duncan Bush's writing.

For myself at this time, I found 'Tartan Army' in *Salt* immediately impressive, and I have clear memories of Bush reading it in public, in his best north Llandaff accent. Today, I admire the poet's vivid portrayal of the Scottish football fans' enthusiasm ('these unmistakable faces of a proletariat') for a match against Wales at Ninian Park, Cardiff, and the police's cynicism directed at those fans: 'they haven't got more sense than that, the bastards' (1986c). This same police attitude was to be used by Bush in his novel *Glass Shot* (1991), but first, his angry writing in *Black Faces, Red Mouths* (1985).

However, there is less concern with Cardiff in both Seren books than might have been expected. 'Cardiff' seems diminished by the time Bush writes 'Coming Back'. Introduced with a quotation from Baudelaire, he writes:

> Every time you come back
> it's shifting again; as if
> the railings had closed in
> on the park; or
>
> the roads had shortened
> their perspectives
>
> (1994a)

This poem might be compared with 'Back?' by T. H. Jones (1921–65), who is almost angrily determined not to return to anywhere, it seems, in Wales, and 'Return to Cardiff' by Dannie Abse (1923–2014), a deliciously melancholic but 'realistic' memory.

Yet Jones writes:

> Of course I'd go back if somebody'd pay me
> To live in my own country
> Like a bloody Englishman.
>
> (1976)

while Abse understands the impossibility of return:

> No sooner than I'd arrived the other Cardiff had gone,
> Smoke in the memory
>
> (1962)

Bush writes in 'Back to Cardiff', from *Salt*:

> I was young here,
> in the truant, errant holiday of youth.
>
> (1986c)

Meanwhile, that 'Saloon Bar Drinker' mutters of 'rooms I rent'. Because home is now near Gravesend or 'near Tilbury Dock' (1986c).

From as early as the poem 'Evening', in *Salt*, Bush was drawn to what he considered the 'melancholia' of life and strove to find images that represented this:

> What does it touch, seeing
> them, these
> men in dark, old suits and cycle-clips,
> with haircuts and haversacks;
> still pedalling slowly from work?
>
> (1986c)

And this, from 'Living', also originally from the closing pages of *Salt*:

Living touches us
strangely, as if with accidental
sadness:
   an old woman
buying a single onion
at a stall
. . .
   I record
these
facts beyond other comment,
only because it might be as if
they never were.

(1986c)

From such early poems we understand why later in life he admitted admiration for Cesare Pavese and W. G. Sebald, as expanded on in chapter 11.

But the now familiar influence of film, cameras, freeze frame and 'slo-mo' is present, and the poet's work in lecturing about film and television, in Newport, in Atlantic College at St Donat's, south Wales, and in Luxembourg, provides a rich source of imagery. This became apparent when I was confronted with Bush's unpublished papers, many of which concern his family and upbringing.

An early poem in which Bush combines history with how we experience its photographic images is 'Movietone', from *Aquarium*. Bush looks at photographs of 'the camps' and Warsaw ghetto, and feels it is as if the figures framed have been:

   arrested
for us
as if held by gunsights.

(1984)

Here there is suspicion of our possible involvement. At least, our complicity. There is no doubt now that what we watch/glance/stare at is for entertainment, aware – willingly or not – that we are a vital part of the whole performance, whether it be sport or war. Yet an important point Bush makes is our general distractedness, or lack of real engagement with what we view. It is difficult to state whether this is our attitude precisely because we understand, at one level, that what we see is not 'real'.

But there is no doubt that the writer could be furiously political when observing other televised spectacles, such as a celebrity death given the grandest possible funeral treatment. 'R.I.P. 6.9.1997', from *Midway*, is about Princess Diana, its searing last line – 'grief turned to karaoke in our veins' (1997a) – a summing up of Elton John and Bernie Taupin's rehashed maudlinisms ('Goodbye, England's Rose' was originally 'Goodbye, Norma Jeane', about Marilyn Monroe). It's the fame that's more real than the famous. This fascination remained with Bush all his life, and makes a sometimes hilarious but ultimately bittersweet last appearance in the novel *Now All the Rage* (2007; see chapter 12).

Also important in both *Aquarium* and *Salt* is the appearance of 'translations' from French and Italian, although Bush is at pains to clarify that these are sometimes versions, the originals manipulated to suit, and also becoming wellsprings for Bush's own poems. As a translator, Bush was no copyist. He loved those originals but felt no awe. He was compelled to leave his own unique mark. For me, 'The Sunflower' by Eugenio Montale is an early highlight. 'Falsetto', again based on Montale's Italian, less so. And Bush's commitment to Cesare Pavese is already in evidence, with versions of 'Fatherhood', 'Revolt' and 'Agony'. Of the Montale translations, he writes: 'I have restructured, reslanted, – and omitted and invented freely – for a poem that is, finally, as much mine as Montale's' (1984). Other poems, he states, are 'literary retellings' rather than translations.

Aquarium's first poem, 'Ulysses Becalmed', uses once again the theme of *Nostos* – a hero's return home after adventure, delay and disaster. The poet seems to be on the beach and takes the opportunity to belittle rivals:

> There is no coming of age
> to their extended, playboy adolescence:
> only age.
>
> (1984)

Bush's returning hero owns up:

> Life was a credit card cashed in on my youth
> against my father's name

Christine Pagnoulle, an assiduous reader of Bush's work, writes online (1995) of a much later poem from *Masks*:

> Bush's impersonations include third-person presentations, as in 'The News of Patroclus.' Here Achilles, succeeding the Odysseus of his earlier 'Ulysses Becalmed,' is referred to in the third person, yet the depth of his grief and the danger that now looms upon him are conjured up from inside. The tolling repetition of the two-word sentence 'He sat' conveys the numbness that follows the blow, and the opening image of 'his silence [hissing] like gas/in the tent' has death lurking around him as it is introduced by 'the messenger's apprehensive / useless, lamentory words.' While suffering makes him feel invulnerable, he stoops on the way out of his tent to adjust 'the loosened sandal at his heel of clay'.

'Summer 1984', a section of its own in *Salt*, is not reprinted in *The Hook*, a selection of Bush's work from his first two publications and his pamphlet, *Black Faces, Red Mouths*. This seems to be a poem Bush believed to be 'unsalvageable', for reprinting in *The Hook*, yet at least he implies he reuses its spirit, if not its vocabulary. Perhaps Bush had abandoned optimism. The poem speaks of:

> In South Wales, in Yorkshire too, and Durham, Kent and Ayrshire
> . . .
> villages no longer
> aggregates of dwellings
> . . .

privatized by television, but
communities again

(1986c)

Instead, what happened during, and then after the strike, was the opposite of 'community' growth. I can recall how Duncan Bush's acquaintance Kim Howells, senior at the time in the South Wales NUM, stated bitterly in an interview on BBC Radio Wales in 1985 that women, notable for their radicalism during the strike, had had to go back to their 'stinking kitchens'. The miners were returning to work and the pits were still being closed.

In light of the facts, I understand why 'Summer 1984' did not become part of *The Hook*. But 'August. Sunday. Gravesend' did. This poem is spare and ominous. The excitements of 'Tartan Army' and the 'in-it-together' spirit of 'Summer 1984' give way to exhaustion. Bush is excellent at exhaustion, whether it's 'sur la plage' or in a Gravesend back garden:

it is like the moment after an explosion.

(1997c)

Maybe this is where Bush abandons his long line and develops a more thoughtful prosody in which individual syllabic sounds are to be savoured (though admittedly 'Sur la Plage' is another sparely constructed piece). Less becomes more, and the Gravesend poem seems to me much better than 'Back to Cardiff', with its unnecessary 'Midsummer' and 'Spring' of the last verse paragraph. The writer does not appear at ease back in Wales.

In fact, *The Hook* closes quietly. 'Hot Estate Sunday', 'Café, Rainy Tuesday Morning' and 'Pull-in' (all originally in *Salt*) display several possible feelings: a sense of betrayal, bewilderment, and a vague idea of something appearing on the horizon. It will be bad news, but as yet is indescribable.

All these poems are built on careful observation – the girl's 'pale bare thigh's faint, blue nebeculae of bruise' in 'Pull-in' (1997c); in 'Café, Rainy Tuesday Morning':

> The boy keeps his cup of
> dregs on the formica table-top
>
> in front of him as if it
> were a ticket for admission;
>
> (1997c)

And, in 'Hot Estate Sunday':

> Sometimes he arrives
> foot-perfect as the bolts go back
> at 7.
> He'll drink tonight until the sky is black.
>
> (1997c)

What was on the horizon? Certainly Margaret Thatcher, but really obsessing Bush at this time was Joseph Stalin, the 'Great Purge' (or the 'Great Terror') and events in Russia before and during the Second World War (see chapter 6). *Salt* was published in 1986, well before the explosion of social media and the internet. For example, Bush joined Facebook, I believe, in 2013.

Both *Aquarium* and *Salt* won Welsh Arts Council literary prizes (in 1984 and 1986), making Duncan Bush a seemingly suddenly arrived heavyweight in the writing scene in Wales.

4

The radical Bush

Duncan Bush was part of a group of 'young' Welsh writers emerging in the 1970s and 1980s who seemed to share a political radicalism. This is reflected not only in what they wrote, but in how that writing was published. The issues that motivated them included nuclear disarmament, Cymraeg (the Welsh language), sexual matters, the apartheid system in South Africa, and environmentalism in all its forms. Frequently, these issues were linked.

The historically minded amongst them would have been aware of the pamphlets of eighteenth-century figures such as Richard Price of Llangeinor and London, and the poetry in manuscript of Iolo Morganwg, which included impersonations and forgeries. Although Iolo was probably unknown to Duncan Bush, (as was possibly Richard Price), this suggests an interesting historical link between such pamphleteers.

The means by which those young writers published led to a resurgence of pamphlet culture and urgent writing about what they considered vital political and social themes. This often bypassed the Arts Council-funded main publishers in Wales and the UK, which until as recently as 2023 felt able to dismiss such often self-published productions as 'vanity' projects (a verbal opinion passed to me by the former publisher at Seren Books).

Undoubtedly these publications often created important social occasions, such as Duncan Bush's reading in Onllwyn, south Wales, in support of the 1984/5 miners' strike. This attracted many people, some of whom found themselves attending their first poetry reading, with Bush experimenting with new poems. These events in their turn became vital expressions of the work of organisations such as CND, Cymdeithas yr Iaith Cymraeg, Friends of the Earth Cymru, Greenpeace and the anti-apartheid groupings.

Central to this is Bush's *Black Faces, Red Mouths* (1985), about the miners' strike, but other committed and determined writers are too numerous to list. They included (in English or bilingually) Peter Finch, Nigel Jenkins, Mike Jenkins, Menna Elfyn, Steve Griffiths, Chris Bendon and Peter Thabit Jones. The host of pamphlets, in no particular order, include Bush's Bedrock Press considerations of the miners' strike; Nigel Jenkins's *Warhead*, about nuclear weapons, printed in 1981 on recycled paper (a symbolic gesture then not easy to achieve) and published by Jenkins's own Megaton Press; Meic Stephens's *Aber Jabber*; Nigel Jenkins and Menna Elfyn's anthology *Glas-Nos* for CND Cymru in 1987; Mike Jenkins's *Rat City*, dealing with Northern Ireland, published by Tony Curtis's Edge Press in Barry in 1979; also in 1979 Nigel Jenkins's *Circus* appeared from Swansea Poetry Workshop. Meanwhile, Tony Curtis's *The Deerslayers* had been published in 1972 by Cwm Nedd Press. Peter Finch was especially prolific in this field, and notable is Finch's magazine for 'new' or 'radical' poetry, *Second Aeon*. This ran for twenty-one issues from 1967 until 1974.

Unignorable is the considerable book-length *Poets Against Apartheid / Beirdd yn Erbyn Apartheid*, edited by Menna Elfyn and Nigel Jenkins. This was launched, significantly, in Clwb Ifor Bach in Cardiff, historically a bastion of Cymraeg. Bush's 'Crocuses' is the first poem included in this volume. This is a harbinger of *The Genre of Silence* (1988; see chapter 6), and concerns the period in Russia of the Great Terror, immediately before the Second World War. It concerns the lives and fears of imprisonment and execution experienced by writers. This is its concluding stanza:

> In the end someone probably
> shot him on a train

going east, or just off it;
and hid the body in the
ground. Here and there his
words come slowly up like
crocuses, in winter.

(Elfyn and Jenkins, 1986)

This anthology was published in 1986, while *Masks*, Bush's first collection to contain the poem, did not appear until 1994.

Duncan's short story 'Boss' (see chapter 16) was also prominent in the anti-apartheid volume, plus his poem 'White Sugar', never republished:

When you buy a pound
of Tate & Lyle's
    white sugar
what
are they really selling you?

They're selling you
  the Pass Laws
They're selling you
  underpaid black workers
They're selling you
  white fear
. . .
They're selling you
  Soweto
They're selling you
  the pound of flesh
They're selling you
  Afrikaaner redneck entrenchment
They're selling you
  The National Party
They're selling you
  torture
They're selling you
  [de]fenestration from the top floor of

an interrogation centre as the latest
form of suicide
They're selling you
Steve Biko's murder
They're selling you
Steve Biko's accidental death
They're selling you
the white judges who whitewashed the police
They're selling you
censorship of press TV radio thought
They're selling you
British investments overseas
They're selling you
Coca Cola Lonrho Rio Tinto Zinc
They're selling you
too many calories
They're selling you
a heart attack at forty-five
They're selling you
holes in your children's teeth
They're selling
You.

(Elfyn and Jenkins, 1986)

'White Sugar' is surprising for Bush, as his writing was rarely explicitly political or polemical. Here, he might be influenced by beat poetry. This rhythmic poetic protest against the sinister interplay of capitalism, consumerism, imperialism and racism is evocative of American beat poetry, particularly Allen Ginsberg's 'America' and 'Howl' (1956), where, as Ginsberg indicated, the repetition of a single word at the beginning of a couplet – such as 'who' in 'Howl', for example, and in Bush's case 'they're' – is used 'to keep the beat, a base to keep measure, return to and take off from again onto another streak of invention'(Ginsberg, 1994) .

But his 'The Last Room: Chabra Camp, 1983' might also be said to be a departure:

at last, in the last
and inmost
room, they find them;
where there had been
no windows to burst through; and
no doorways left. Only
the corners
they had pressed
together into; like the refugees
they had been; in a second atrocious
silence where the flies
buzzed, stopped: huddled
together, as they had
been, in this
farmost chamber of all

(Bush, 1985b)

This appeared in *Poetry Wales* in 1985 and remains uncollected. What's striking is that as the poem progresses it acquires the style of a filmed documentary, as if a camera follows the subjects until discovery of their deaths.

Unexpected, perhaps, is Bush's absence from *Glas-Nos* (1987), an anthology compiled for CND Cymru by Nigel Jenkins and Menna Elfyn. This seems especially disappointing, as a flurry of poems about environmental issues, such as 'The Sunday the Power Went Off', 'After Chernobyl' and 'Just a Few Things Daddy Knows About Ice', would appear in *Masks* in 1994. But this might have been the period when Bush 'did not write a poem for a year', while engaged in writing *Glass Shot* (quoted by Pagnoulle, 1995). Environmental as they are, and predictive of cataclysm, these poems are all the more effective for the poet introducing his 'five-year-old elder son', father and son counting the seconds together through the ominous 'sulphur-violet dimness' (1994).

Yet still Bush must have recourse to films. 'The Sunday the Power Went Off' has the image of a thunder crack:

Like a rifle-shot amplifying
down a badlands canyon

in movies, the one-off perfect shot
bringing a man unexpectedly down
forever, though the sunlight

unimpaired, the reel
unfinished

(1994)

I compare this 'perfect shot' to the 'hell of a shot' Wesley Rees Ball fires in Vietnam, in 'Are There Still Wolves in Pennsylvania?', that murders a sixteen-year-old girl (see chapter 10). As a cinema buff, Bush might have been aware of the 1973 Hollywood film *Badlands*, a retelling of a killing spree. This image is reminiscent of another rifle-shot Bush imagines, his character Stew Boyle, in *Glass Shot* (1991), expecting retribution as he escapes after the theft of a handbag and 'a bullet exactly midway between the shoulder blades' (see chapter 8).

Meanwhile in 1995 Seren Books published *Green Agenda: Essays on the Environment of Wales*, edited by Robert Minhinnick, for Friends of the Earth Cymru. The launch events for this were sponsored by the Countryside Council for Wales and Dŵr Cymru. This is clear indication of radical issues belatedly becoming mainstream. Regular literary events were organised via FoE Cymru for writers who included Peter Finch, Ifor Thomas and Hilary Llewellyn Williams.

Duncan Bush appeared at one of these at the Porthcawl Hotel in the late 1980s. He also performed, along with a host of other authors, including Dai Smith, Nigel Jenkins, Peter Finch and Tony Curtis, at an environmental benefit night on 13 March, 1986 in Cardiff. I am in possession of photographs of Bush performing here. Thus, organisations such as CND Cymru and Friends of the Earth Cymru themselves had (belatedly) understood that concepts such as 'peace' and 'sustainability' had little meaning without 'artistic' expression or interpretation. Some of this is touched upon by Jane Aaron and M. Wynn Thomas in their joint essay (2003).

Undoubtedly research should be done into this febrile period of political and social commitment and publishing, and the links established between the writing communities and Cymdeithas yr Iaith Cymraeg, CND, Friends of the Earth Cymru (especially its campaign against opencast coalmining) and the Wales Anti-Apartheid Movement.

Nigel Jenkins, Menna Elfyn, Duncan Bush and many others were aware of the samizdat tradition of publication, and this has always been a possibility for those with radical messages. Benjamin Ramm has written of the samizdat tradition: 'It was under Khrushchev's rule that *samizdat* gained prominence in the Soviet Union, as the production of material not in accordance with official ideology no longer carried a death sentence' (2017). Ramm dates 1956 and Krushchev's so-called 'secret speech' as a turning point in the attitude in Russia to critics of the state.

Bush especially wrote of the mortal dangers of any unapproved publication during the pre-Second World War Great Terror in Russia. This, from 'Geranium', in *The Genre of Silence*, in the persona of the fictional poet Victor Bal:

> The life that was
> or could have been is
> over now. You must, I tell myself,
> live slow and sure and silent
>
> and within yourself. Act
> blind and deaf and
> dumb. Above all, dumb.
> Shape words, but give forth
>
> silence. Put out neither
> fruit nor flower nor leaf.
> You must look like a stone,
> but live. Like a cactus.

> This poem is written in Bal's notebook in purple ink.
> Underneath Bal has added the following in pencil – and in such a way that it is not clear if it is a prose afterthought about the poem or a new last line for it:
> Not even that. The lichen on a rock.

(1988)

How similarly powerful this is to 'Crocuses', uncollected until *Masks* (1994), but for me the better poem.

Victor Bal is the central figure in Bush's *The Genre of Silence*, discussed in chapter 6. In this novel, Bush provides Bal's 'biography': 'A Brief Life', from his birth in 1898 to his 'disappearance' in the surmised 1938.

In 2023, writer John Barnie was seeking newspaper samizdat publication, based on Phil Cope's *I Dig Margam* newspaper from 2021. In Wales, such treatises, religious, artistic or political, in both languages, are myriad and have an honourable history. The collaboration with graphic artists and typesetters should also be noted, in Bush's case with John Uzzell Edwards, a colleague from Newport College of Art, who provided the artwork for both *Aquarium* and *Salt*. Artist John Selway worked on *The Genre of Silence*.

This publishing depended on a tiny hard core of committed individuals. I don't believe Duncan Bush and Nigel Jenkins always agreed with one other (this might have led to Bush's absence from the *Glas-Nos* anthology), but they are crucially linked during this period. Both men are anyway associated by their appearance together in *Three Young Anglo-Welsh Poets* (1974), and by their similar ages, Bush born in 1946 and Jenkins in 1949.

When Bush republished his first two volumes, together with his miners' strike poems, as *The Hook* in 1997, he took pains to recount his reaction to the strike – or, should it be, to televisual images of the 'battle of Orgreave':

> I still recall standing up out of my chair in astonishment and horror at seeing a man I knew, Philip James of Coelbren, take a blow to the head from

> an officer on horseback and then, while stunned and holding the visibly bleeding wound, suffer arrest on national television by other officers.
>
> It was later established that the true sequence of events had been reversed in a BBC editing suite: in reality, the mounted police (in full riot-control uniform, with shields and batons) had charged into the ranks of miners (on foot, unarmed, and in daps and t-shirts), who had fallen back in broken order and only, at that point, began throwing whatever missiles came to hand. (1997c)

Duncan Bush was happy also to support the Valley and Vale Community Arts initiative, under the directorship of Phil Cope. In its time, this was a radical and successful venture, with bases in Barry and Bridgend county borough, south Wales, where community plays were presented. Phil Cope recalls collaborating with Bush:

> In the late 1980s, Duncan Bush worked on a number of writing projects for Valley and Vale, Wales' largest community arts team with bases in Blaengarw, Tondu, Bettws and Barry. We regularly created large-scale community plays, often with a cast in the hundreds performing at a variety of sites, both indoors and out.
>
> Duncan worked as the dramaturge on one of these about the hardships of coalmining in the Garw Valley which once 'boasted' six pits. He worked with me, director, and the local performers to develop a script, and while he struggled, as many 'professional' artists often do, with the tensions surrounding the 'ownership' of co-authored work – I remember a heated debate about the size and placement of his name on the poster – his understandings of the effects of the coal industry both on the land and on its people, and his powerful, gritty and insightful language transformed the project. (pers. corr. 2023)

Bush's radicalism is highlighted in his writings about the 1984/5 miners' strike, and the poems of *Black Faces, Red Mouths*. It continued to be a feature in his work for much of his life. The next chapter turns to another theme that runs through this work: his attitude to Wales.

5

'Gwlad, Gwlad'? Duncan Bush and Wales[1]

Duncan Bush could be brutal about Wales. Being Welsh, he felt this was allowable. And necessary. The poem, 'Gwlad, Gwlad' first appeared in *Salt*, and he chose to republish it in *The Hook* (1997), his combined poems from his first three collections. I always thought the poem amusingly harsh on his compatriots. But reading it again, perhaps the last lines:

> a people so stiffnecked
> yea, verily unto sullenness,
> they'll duck to advantage
> but look up to no man

might be read as a national compliment (1997c).

Ian Gregson, in a letter to *Poetry Wales*, titled 'Transplanted (Duncan) Bush', quotes Bush himself from an interview with the magazine in 2002:

> There's a kind of fascism, overt or merely sleeping; in all these narrow, pugnacious forms of nationalism – whether it's institutionalized as in National Front in France and the Northern League in Italy; or just the blocked-barrel bigotry of the bar-stool patriots we know in Wales, whose only programme is Anglophobia allied to a generalized disgruntlement; and their counterparts in England who love the pound and hate 'asylum-seekers'. (2005)

Because 'identity' is a national obsession in Wales, Duncan returned to it frequently. In his unpublished papers, he writes:

> For the Bushes, the distance between us and 'the Welsh' was maintained and honoured, like a token of ancient religious faith, in the fact that my father's family had originated in the West Country (with a faint trace of Irish blood rumoured on my paternal grandmother's side).

In this context it is interesting to note M. Wynn Thomas's characterisation of Duncan Bush's writing as coming from 'West Britain', in *Corresponding Cultures: The Two Literatures of Wales* (1999), and also the poem 'At St Mary Redcliffe', which concerns his West Country ancestors, and appeared in *Poetry Wales* (2003b) (see chapter 14 in this volume). Also, in 'Wales's American Dreams', a chapter in his volume *Corresponding Cultures*, M. Wynn Thomas writes:

> Bush's Welshness is, in fact, very much that of one who feels himself to be a West Briton. And although he announces 'I'm no patriot and I'm proud of it', his concept of America obviously originates in his angry identification with the class-ridden, ethnically divided West Britain (south Wales) of his childhood and youth in the Llandaff area of Cardiff... In the intermingling of Welsh and West Country ancestry in his own family background, Bush identifies the kind of meld that the melting-pot culture of the United States has helped him see as the process that also brought modern Britain into existence. Further, in the egalitarianism of the United States he discerns the lineaments of the classless society, which, he believes, the British working class vainly dreamt of establishing at the end of the Second World War. (1999)

Duncan Bush's unpublished account quoted above continues: '*Yet the idea of being English was somehow equally unacceptable – at least, in this post-war period when ... the American entertainment industry was a ubiquitous component of ordinary lives and Britishness itself seemed somehow second-rate.*' And he adds: 'Anti-British feeling is a familiar concept; but it's not always recognized how much it's always existed as a natural undercurrent among its own citizenry.' Bush's interview by Richard Poole in *Poetry Wales*, of which Poole was then editor, includes descriptions of the writer's feelings (some negative, but some not) about his home country, and also what he aspired to in the 'role for the writer': 'it's true that I detest the comforting, the cosy, the homiletic in writing' (1992a). And he answers amusingly when asked about his relationship with Wales, stating he felt 'unimpressed, embarrassed' by the national 'relationship' with the leek, as viewed on his visits to Welsh international rugby matches. Bush would certainly believe 'nationalist' sentiment, as sometimes expressed about Wales, fell under the 'homiletic' here (a homily, I suggest, in his meaning, being a moralising instruction on how to behave or what to think, or how to vote).

Thus he had high standards for what a writer should aspire to: the countless writers written about or translated by Duncan Bush include Paul Valéry, Rimbaud, Baudelaire, Saul Bellow, John Updike, Siegfried Sassoon, Osip Mandelstam, Isaac Babel and Cesare Pavese. Very much their own people. And a list, entirely male, and of its time.

Yet if the Welsh could sometimes feel castigated by Bush, I suggest critics read his introduction to *Picture: Welsh Poets* (1987), a gorgeous production of Newport College of Art student Stuart Smith's photographs. Bush was its commissioning editor. All but two of the poets and writers are male – and we must make what we will of that. The changes, thankfully, have been seismic. But the book production, from a youthful Seren Books, is superb, and the young Stuart Smith treated regally.

Bush's idea was to commission Smith, who was studying photography and graphic design, to take photographs of Welsh writers, and for those writers to inscribe their poetry or prose upon the photographs themselves, and date the occasion. The poems and prose are printed, more legibly, alongside. The self-chosen photograph of Bush has him resembling some academic bruiser, befitting someone who had worked as a gasfitter, drain-layer and at numerous out-of-doors practical jobs.

In his introduction, Bush writes very clearly about 'Wales' and nationality. I think it one of his most thoughtful utterances on the subject, and unknown to many who considered him 'anti-Welsh':

> It is by no means an accidental irony that the comparatively small lexicon of the Welsh language provides two adjectives for 'Welsh' – 'Cymreig' (for Welsh nationality) and 'Cymraeg' (of or in the Welsh language) – whereas all the semantic wealth of English, gives only one, an adjective therefore condemned to ambiguity. Is a Welsh poet only one who writes in Welsh? Or can it be one who happens to be born in Wales or whose work may in some way relate to Wales and Welsh experience? It is to avoid this ambiguity, and in lieu of a more gracious term, that the unfortunate compound 'Anglo-Welsh' has arisen – a term which many of the writers in this book would certainly object to, for its air of editorial pigeon holing, for its defensiveness; for its already colonized implications . . . even for its suggestion that their nationality itself is in some sense an area of ambiguity or doubt. (1987)

Bush went on to suggest that the use of the word 'Welsh' in *Picture: Welsh Poets* 'will no doubt seem a provocation to some . . . It is used here . . . not necessarily provocatively but with a straightforwardness about the simple happenstance of nationality which it is actually appropriate and essential to assert'.

Picture: Welsh Poets, from 1987, might be compared with *Anglo-Welsh Literature: An Illustrated History*, by Roland Mathias, from 1986. Both volumes are from Poetry Wales Press (which became Seren Books), but they demonstrate the rapid change in sensibility as to what might constitute a Welsh (or Anglo-Welsh) writer.

Meanings and definitions were changing before the eyes of writers and their publishers alike at this time. Some critics were discomfited. Thus the latter book, from 1986, already appears dated, indeed meaningless. Yet in its time it was a valiant attempt to describe a puzzling scene. Mathias describes Duncan Bush as having not yet 'demonstrated the same concentration of interest' in Wales as other writers named (1986) . And he ends his brief survey with the question 'Is Anglo-Welsh writing in any meaningful sense of that term, likely to survive the century?' (a similar sentiment to that voiced in his foreword for *Green Horse*, see chapter 3).

The answer was, and remains, 'no'. What changed were appreciations of what 'Wales' was, is, and might be. I recall Duncan writing to congratulate me when I became editor of *Poetry Wales* in 1997, a position I retained until January 2009. My first issue coincided with the second Welsh devolution vote in autumn, 1997, and we held up the editorial until it was announced that Wales had said 'Yes' (by the slimmest of margins). The editorial was titled 'A Country that Said "Yes"'.

I have no idea how Bush voted, but can guarantee that he was delighted to become a columnist in a magazine that propounded such views. My editorial principle was never to define 'Wales' (or 'poetry'), as I believed it was unhealthy, unnecessary and impossible to do so. And Duncan Bush was not concerned whether critics or readers felt him to be a Welsh or Anglo-Welsh writer. What he always craved was to be recognised as a 'European' author.

In his foreword, as editor, to *Picture: Welsh Poets*, titled 'The Portrait of the Artist', Bush writes: 'The true portrait, like the true poem, is an act of dissent and secrecy' (1987). This I think excellent, in that it deepens the art in question (but as to 'true portrait . . . true poem', that also must remain indefinable). Yet, in the conclusion of this foreword, dated 18 May 1987, he is adamant about the description 'Anglo-Welsh', which he clearly found dismissive: 'The truth may be that the term . . . in seeking to avoid all ambiguity and paradox, has instead helped foster and promote the narrowness of a division' (1987).

Bush could be hard on the Welsh, and sometimes this attracted an exasperated response. This, from Daniel G. Williams in his *Wales Unchained*: 'but it is disappointing to find a writer of Bush's sensitivity forcing his readers into a corner with his finger-jabbing pronouncements on the alleged narrow-minded provincialism of modern Wales' (2015). However, the English are not spared by Bush. His column in *Poetry Wales* (consisting of four separate essays, under my editorship, 1997–2008) turned, early on, to English tourism in France. This, from 'Francophilia': 'what is it about the whining complacencies of estuarine English that raises so much hatred in the rest of us? Snobbish or not . . . it's hard to like this new generation of British tourists, with their near-colonialist attitudes to property in France' (2002a). That 'the rest of us' is surely significant. Yes, anti-(a sort of) English, but also anti-British. Yes, above all, Bush could be anti-British. This is evident in the eighteen-page autobiographical essay 'Lash LaRue and the River of Adventure' (*Midway*), which was first published in *Planet: The Welsh Internationalist*, a journal that has always prided itself on its 'independent Wales' philosophy. Bush wrote:

> Bitter expression of the (post-war) period's pro-American and anti-British sentiment was voiced by a friend of my father's, a plumber who had actually worked in the US. After describing a booming transatlantic economy and an enviable standard of living, fed by higher salaries and lower prices, he reached a portentous summary. 'Don', he told my father, 'we've been hoodwinked all our lives'. (1997a)

This friend of Bush's father possibly means 'hoodwinked' in both political and cultural senses.

A little earlier in this essay, Bush had written about anti-Britishness:

> *At the time I'm describing this was a natural result of six years of war on a working-class population exhausted from that experience* ... In fact, in our household in Llandaff North, British films were despised, almost on principle. This was not only because of the patriotic atmosphere many of them had ... The class system they embodied was ... ludicrously anachronistic. (1997a)

And here he seems to share the opinions of critic and author Peter Stead, as in the latter's essay 'Wales in the Movies':

> Whatever the reason, Welsh audiences like other regional and working-class audiences in Britain accepted the fact that they would not see themselves in the movies unless it was in the guise of music-hall types brought in occasionally as humble policemen or railway porters to relieve the predominantly middle-class metropolitan and middle-brow drama. (1986)

In his undated papers, Bush writes:

> The list of other ranks from the J. Arthur Rank payroll counted among life's natural ground-crew: they were chock-pullers and batmen. However heroic

> they were too in their unassuming way, their role was a partly comic one and they spoke Cockney or Welsh or Glaswegian. But it has ever been thus, since Fluellen and MacMorris.

And from his same essay, quoting approvingly, Peter Stead writes: 'Tony Garnett was once to observe that "to be an Englishmen in the film industry is to know what it's like to be colonised"' (1986).

Born in Barry in 1943, and becoming an academic in Swansea University, Stead was clearly Bush's type of Welshman: cosmopolitan, wry. Undoubtedly they were aware of one another's writings. Peter Stead also writes, in 'Wales in the Movies': 'As much as anything it reminds us of how severe was the cultural crisis in Britain and how urgently the new departures in popular culture were needed. Welshness was hopelessly parodied in the movies' (1986). And it is not difficult to imagine Bush himself writing the following, also from Stead's essay:

> [A] perpetual desire to play Hollywood at its own game did more than anything to prevent the development of a truly national (i.e. Welsh) film style. The contrast was with Italy where in the devastation of the post-war years a new breed of directors just went into the streets to make neo-realistic films that took the art-houses of the world by storm. The films of Rossellini and de Sica suggested that perhaps the British failure was as much artistic as commercial. (1986)

Stead is fascinatingly similar to Bush in terms of his equivocation, indeed disappointment, about Wales. I find this ambivalence clear in his biography *Richard Burton: So Much, So Little* (1991), in which the author creates a picture of Burton not through his fame but out of his 'Welshness'. The title, as far as Stead is concerned, says it all, and, at only 130 pages, the book seems to gutter out, similarly to Burton's early death at 58.

I always expected Bush, in his prose especially, to make reference to baseball, as during his life in Wales this was a well-known Cardiff working-class sport. It flourished because of a profound American influence on Cardiff culture. There exist cultural allusions, chiefly in Welsh popular music, for example, 'The Baseball Song' by Cardiff folk group the Hennessys, from their 1984 album *Cardiff After Dark* (a title deliberately chosen for its local pronunciation), stressing the Cardiff vowels which I was always familiar with, including within Duncan Bush's north Llandaff accent, and which he might have occasionally stressed, as a badge of . . . what? Working-class credentials? Or his 'Welshness'? This writer believed in fluidity of genres. But also identities, including his own.

Yet I do not believe Duncan wrote about baseball, despite a preponderance of Cardiff baseball teams being based in Splott and Grangetown, home of Stew Boyle in *Glass Shot* (1991), and thus familiar to its author. Instead, Bush composed descriptive poetry and Facebook entries about ostensibly middle-class, but also Australian cricket (see chapters 9 and 13 in this volume).

Duncan Bush frequently in interviews said he believed writers should not toe a party line. I'd say he opposed any orthodoxy wherever he discovered it. And he seemed to find it in Wales. For me, Bush's real subject here is 'class' and not 'Wales' or 'England' or an amorphous 'Britain'. In the novel *Glass Shot*, leading character Stew Boyle complains: 'All you can get in this part of Grangetown is S4C, Ess Pedwar Eck. Amateur Night. In Welsh most of the time. (About as much use to me or the average citizen of the capital as an *Echo* [the popular local evening paper] in [B]raille.)' (1991).

By the time he published *Aquarium* (1984), Bush had the reputation of being someone who spoke his mind. Bush's feelings about nationalism and certain nationalists are also found in 'Tristia: A Poem for St. David's Day', in *The Hook*: 'those paravail [a frequently used Bushian word] churls' (1997c). And here it comes again, this from an unpublished and undated section of memoir (surely much later in composition): 'Beyond [Cardiff] lay Wales, a hinterland of envious paravails – "Boyos", "Shonnies", "Sheep-shaggers" – who lived on mountainsides or at their foot in huddled strings of dirty villages; a place known with grandiose unfamiliarity as "Up the Valleys".'

Most writers grow fond of particular words. These days it's easier to shrug at Bush's fear of any form of 'nationalism' but from the same text we learn that 'for anyone born into a working class family on the northern edge of Cardiff (in April, 1946), cultural identity, whether in a collective or personal sense, was always an equivocal concept'. And we should never doubt Bush's use of irony, especially when he believes, indeed hopes, that he might be taken literally. He loved to stir up outrage.

The miners' strike, 1984/5, was important for many Welsh writers, but especially Duncan Bush. He and his partner Annette Weaver had purchased in 1984 a property in the village of Ynyswen, in the extreme north of the Swansea and Neath valleys, at the foot of Bannau Brychieiniog (then the Brecon Beacons). This was very much part of the south Wales coalfield, close to villages such as Abercraf, Banwen and Onllwyn. Bush was angered by the government reaction to the strike and its subsequent closure of mines in Wales and the UK, and threw himself into the miners' struggle with the best means available to him: his poetry. But he also organised poetry reading events which became highly social and political occasions. He brought out *Black Faces, Red Mouths* in 1985 and collects six of the poems in this self-published pamphlet in *The Hook*, which was otherwise a reprinting of much of his *Salt* and *Aquarium* collections. He wrote, of these miners' strike poems: 'Sometimes, in order to avoid self-revisionism, a poet should simply let his work bear witness to what he saw and thought at the time – leaving the testimony intact, as if made under oath' (1997c). He wanted these poems in the public eye. A major part of his response to the strike was the forming of Bedrock Press in Ynyswen, located at his home, Godre Waun Oleu. Deliberately choosing to live at that time in Ynyswen might be construed as an act of class solidarity.

'In the Aftermath' is a kind of summing up and attempt at understanding the causes and results of the strike. But maybe the most significant writing is 'Onllwyn, West Glamorgan, 1985', ending with Bush's description of the contempt displayed by the state for miners, their families and their environment:

Not
even bulldozing or leaving the
bought seed to grass over
. . .
the mountainous geology of waste.

(1997c)

In *The Hook* Bush writes of these poems: 'What they allude to was, for many people, part of the most intense, cataclysmic and divisive emergency to take place in domestic politics in Britain since the Second World War'. Undoubtedly, the strike had a huge impact on Welsh consciousness. Yet Duncan Bush abhorred 'nationalist' political sentiments. In an unpublished memoir-like prose work, he writes of the almost self-delusionary idea of owning one's own property. And he expands this:

> Of course, the sense of belonging usually extends in a wider territorial sense. Most individuals are anxious to claim origins in a town or city, a region or nationality. But I seem to have been endowed with less of an instinct for collective identity too. The intense tribalism that raises some men to heights of exultation or sinks them into depression because of the result of a horse race in Siena or a football match in Manchester is foreign to me. But then, I've always secretly preferred that as a status: to have the mystique of the foreigner. Perhaps that's all it is, ultimately; a matter of vanity.

So, let's be frank. Duncan Bush did not hate Wales. What he hated were expressions of nationalism, which throughout his life he had considered ridiculous. There's no clearer expression of this than in 'Tristia' (reprinted in *The Hook*), Bush describing himself:

At one – the odd
sporting fixture aside –
with Dr Johnson as to what is
'the last refuge of the scoundrel'.

(1997c)

Yet, Bush has been fortunate to attract the attention of perspicacious critics. Ian Gregson, in his letter to *Poetry Wales*, attempts to comment on this shape-shifting writer:

> Bush's internationalist postmodernism needs to be qualified at every turn by [his] sense of vestigial rootedness; these two are in a constant and unresolved dialogue which interrogates what national identity has come to mean. International voices speak in Bush's poems – Americans, a Russian, a South African mercenary – but he turns back constantly to south Wales. This backward turn is not just geographical but historical: Bush repeatedly returns to a postwar Cardiff and sounds an elegiac note which half shames him because such 'private tristia' might associate him with yobbish and self-serving 'patrioteers'. (2005)

And Gregson continues, perhaps identifying any critic's conundrum when writing about this author:

> Bush's sensibility has been formed by experiences which link him – despite his public statements – to an 'Anglo-Welsh' poetic.
>
> This helps to account for a strand in his work which otherwise sits oddly with his postmodernism. For, alongside his sophisticated self-reflexivity, there are surprising moments of regret and nostalgia which place him in unexpected poetic company: his style is very different, but the preoccupation with loss is something he shares with other members of an 'Anglo-Welsh' tradition such as R. S. Thomas or Gillian Clarke, and very much not with postmodernists such as John Ashbery and Paul Muldoon. (2005)

Duncan Bush's very real 'link . . . to an "Anglo-Welsh" poetic' is looked at throughout this volume, as are the concepts of 'exile' and 'self-exile'. And Bush certainly aligned himself with the striking Welsh miners' cause – surely an act of class solidarity. Into that struggle he pledged what, after his family, was most important to him: his art.

This chapter has discussed Bush's attitude with Wales; the next turns to his wider political interests, focusing on his first novel, *The Genre of Silence*, set in Stalinist Russia.

Note

1 'Gwlad, Gwlad' is a quotation from 'Mae Hen Wlad Fy Nhadau', the national anthem of Wales. It is also the title of a Duncan Bush poem.

6

The Genre of Silence (1988)

> 'Good novelists extend not only their own fictional universe but the possibility of fictional forms.' (2004d)

The Genre of Silence is a 100-page volume of prose and poetry by Duncan Bush, published by Seren in 1988. Bush and its publishers always referred to it as a 'novel'. The back cover of the first edition explains:

> Duncan Bush's new work brings to life, at times painfully, the work of the Russian poet, Victor Bal, who 'disappeared' under Stalinism. This surprising and original new book recalls the period by an intermingling of history and fiction which imaginative writers have always understood but that historians have rarely admitted.

I pause at that 'intermingling'. Victor Bal is an entirely fictional character, although created by Bush's readings of Russian history. And Isaac Babel, another character, who exists in memory, including that of Bal, was very much a real-life writer, whose collected stories have recently been published.[1]

On two occasions academics inquired of me, as then editor of *Poetry Wales*, whether they might write about the book, with special regard to Bush's biographical detailing of the life of the vanished poet, Victor Bal. Didn't these critics, I wondered, understand that Victor Bal was a fictional creation? And that the poems of Victor

Bal were written by someone else, that person being Duncan Bush? When I broke the news to the critics they did not, as I expected, wish to write about *The Genre of Silence* itself. They apologised for their stupidity – not that I considered them stupid, as the book fails to make entirely clear that Bal is a fictional character. Bush provides Bal with a biography in the section 'A Brief Life', informing readers that he 'was born on January 3, 1898, in the Kolomna district of Petersburg. The son of a doctor, he attended the Tenishev School (as Mandelstam and Nabokov had a few years earlier)' (1988b).

Things might have been complicated for the critics by the back-cover quotation from Osip Mandelstam's translator, Clarence Brown: 'Even non-persons have biographies, but it is extraordinarily difficult to establish them.' Non-persons? Anyone who has read *1984* will think they know what that means: non-persons can be fictional but also *real* people whose identities have been erased by a political system. Victor Bal was not a 'non-person' but a 'never-been person'. However, for me, 'non-persons' are real people. One such real person who became a 'non-person' was Isaac Emmanuelovich Babel. But Victor Bal did not disappear into the Gulag or behind the walls of Moscow's Butyrka prison, because he never lived.

Certain poems by Duncan Bush seemed to fit in with the overall intentions of this novel. 'Crocuses' was one such, published in *Masks* but surely belonging in this, Bush's first novel. 'The Galley' is another. This first appeared in the edited collection *Picture: Welsh Poets* (1987) (see previous chapter). It is described by Richard Poole in his essay, 'Duncan Bush's Personae' , as having 'the force of a concentrated moral fable' (1992b). I leave the reader to agree or not with Poole's words. Here is the whole of 'The Galley', said to be the work of Victor Bal, the poem classified in *The Genre of Silence* as amongst Bal's 'early poems':

> Let some have whips and wear uniform;
> Let some have oars and wear rag. Let these
> be more. So have them shackled
> at ankle and wrist. Let the galley

move. The immense effort of shifting
inert mass through sea is well known.
A strange thing is, those
in the uniform think it's the strokes
of the whip which achieve it.

(1988b)

Reality, memory, art, identity. As I become older, I recognise how they blend. Which is dangerous. Surely one answer to this woolliness is to listen, as Victor Bal did, to the atmosphere of the Russian pine forest.

I believe Duncan Bush's experience of the Welsh Union of Writers (WUW) in the 1980s influenced *The Genre of Silence*. The Union was created in summer 1982, and Bush joined two years later. By 1986 he had edited a conference report/anthology, *On Censorship*. Maybe it was Bush's idea that this conference theme be adopted, as it clearly fitted in with his research for and writing of *The Genre of Silence*.

Bush edited this anthology under the chairmanship of broadcaster John Morgan. I have photographs of the 'committee' for that conference, held in Dyffryn Gardens, near Cardiff, in 1986. Bush, wearing an anorak, stands beside (among others) John Osmond, Robin Reeves, Harri Pritchard Jones and John Morgan himself. The conference was sponsored by HTV, Isoflex Liquid Rubber and South Glamorgan County Council. I also possess two photographs of Duncan delivering a lecture, with the assistance of a filmed contribution via a television.

Duncan Bush was an unlikely union member, not that I know many 'typical' members of literary unions. (Or do I?) But Bush's experiences of the WUW might have confirmed certain prejudices: that not all writers are of equal talent, and certain of them are not reluctant to accept a general invitation to perform their work. These invitations involved readings of 'poetry', at the 'open mics', which were amongst the most eagerly anticipated of WUW events at annual conferences. Such readings were organised because they appeared to guarantee a decent conference attendance and thus a successful event that might keep funding agencies happy. (This type of energetic open mic-er is now familiar to most literary people who use social media.)

I believe it was these WUW events that fed into *The Genre of Silence*. At least, what is obvious is Bush's distaste for writers who conformed to prevailing orthodoxy or parroted a party line. This is clearest in 'Writers' Union Building, Moscow, 1937', which is depicted as 'Free Hotel? Or tomb of living writers?'. Especially:

> This year, they tell me, members are
> sporting Ukrainian embroidered shirts
> when they herd to conferences –
>
> sheep in peasants' clothing. Sheep
> milling for the microphone
> like wolves. And, like wolves, getting
>
> stronger the longer you run.
>
> (1988b)

That 'you' is interesting. The wolves are chasing prey. Is the prey Bal or Babel? Or Bush?

In the WUW, the prevailing orthodoxy was sympathy for an independent Wales. I shared it. Duncan Bush did not. I also believe he was appalled by the standard of some of the spoken literary offerings he heard at WUW conferences and determined to use this dismay to make a far wider point. He does this, I feel, successfully in *The Genre of Silence*. Bush could be adamant about writers. In his Richard Poole interview in *Poetry Wales* (Poole, 1992a), he stated: 'it shouldn't be the group or party line – the political version of the Received Idea – which emerges in their work'. No, Bush did not have much regard for the majority of his fellow union writers. I imagine he thought they lacked what he considered essential for the true writer, and which he puts into the mind of Victor Bal – an 'insistence on a poet's own creative autonomy and self-critical sense'. This is most clearly expressed in *The Genre of Silence* in 'The Muscle Under the Tongue':

> Poets? Writers? Hardly.
> But there's no surer way to fame
> for camp dogs: licking the hand
> that feeds them space
> to do so, prints their name.
>
> (1988b)

Victor Bal (maybe fictionally) and Isaac Babel (maybe factually) describe conditions for Russian writers in the 1930s, and especially in 1938, at the height of the Great Purge or Great Terror. Bal's 'poem in draft' 'Geranium' outlines how a writer then must live (see extract in chapter 4). As it turns out (Bush writes), 'not even silence is enough to guarantee survival. But for Bal as for other writers in the Soviet Union during the Thirties, silence seems to represent the last integrity possible' (1988b).

All of Victor Bal's poetry is by Duncan Bush, while 'the genre of silence' is originally a phrase coined by Isaac Babel that became a way of life, a belief, a philosophy, a blueprint of how, maybe, to survive.[2]

Yet silence could not save Babel. Bush states in the book that he is 'presumed to have died, in unrecorded circumstances, in a concentration camp in 1939 or 40' (1988b). However, other sources claim he died on 27 January, 1940, shot by firing squad after a one-day trial (for example, Freidin, 2025). Yet according to the early official Soviet version, Isaac Babel died in the Gulag on 17 March, 1941. Peter Constantine, the British-American writer who translated Babel's complete writings in 2002 and 2003, has described his execution as 'one of the great tragedies of 20th century literature' (2002).

The 'A Brief Life' section of the novel ends with this statement: 'In the words of Nadezhda Mandelstam, with the example of her own husband in mind: People can be killed for poetry here – a sign of unparalleled respect – because they are still capable of living by it' (1988b).

Why should anyone read *The Genre of Silence*? Undoubtedly for the spare, Bushian poetry. The novel also contains always adept, occasionally breathtaking phrase-making that we have learned to expect from Duncan Bush. I find this writer is capable of lines and images that have the power to raise the hairs on the back of the neck. Thus: 'But few of us, educated or not, can talk with the slow and ungainsayable authority of Voloshin, with those Tartar eyes and his skull still blue from headlice and his beard of iron filings' (1988b).

'Greatest Welsh novel'? I wonder what Bush would make of the challenge to nominate this, from the entire history of Welsh publishing. I imagine he would have felt it a wheeze worthy of the old WUW. But I accepted it, writing about *The Genre of Silence*, as I had seen that the other choices already made were, I considered, expected and conservative. For myself, it would have been more straightforward if I had chosen Bush's second novel, *Glass Shot*, frankly a relentless monologue or soliloquy, praised by Hilary Mantel's comment on the cover, and a more conventionally gripping novel than the earlier book (see chapter 8).

The Genre of Silence contains some admittedly short scene settings as the author establishes his context. But with the opening section, 'In the Pine Forest', we are immediately into the meat of the book. Bush depicts Victor Bal, who has been labouring (sawing tree trunks) and thinking, only thinking so far, about a poem and its first line. This compares the mood in Russia of that time to the immense, ominous silence there is in its pine forests. Surely, the authorities couldn't do anything about *thinking* of writing a poem? Could they? Of working on the poem's music and rhythm in the poet's head? Yet for Bal this might prove the poem 'that would kill him' (1988b).

'Greatest Welsh Novel' was a competition created in 2014 by *Wales Arts Review*. *The Genre of Silence* didn't come close to garnering enough support. Also, it could be devoured in an afternoon. But this would be a dismissal. A rapid reading would diminish its power. Certain of the poems within it, notably 'The Leader', 'Peasant' and 'Night, Day', evoke an abominable period of Russian history, and might encourage enquiry into what is going on now (2024) in Ukraine. These poems must be reread. Whereas others, 'For Marina', for example, with their lyrical sense of loss, make those events even more poignant, as Bush outlines a few of the marvellous particularities of what is lost to Babel (in actuality) and Victor Bal (in imagination).

> I love the way your big toes point
> down the bed when you come –
>
> most of all in summer, when again
> we can lie on, not under,
>
> the strawberry-flowered quilt
> in the full afternoon
>
> naked as the new-born
> mice under the floorboarding
>
> (1988b)

Any attentive reading of Bush's work provides evidence that certain images and ideas are used in both his prose and poetry, as if being tested out. Or refined. Or as experiments. The prose and poetry seed one another. There are links between all of the main characters in Bush's novels, and thus it is impossible and unnatural to demarcate the genres (and the books) the author created. Nothing comes from nowhere.

His author's biography at Seren once stated he was 'currently completing a novel about a politician in the Sarkozy government' in France. Subsequent to *The Genre of Silence*, Bush published two novels: *Glass Shot* (1991) and *Now All the Rage* (2007), concerned with how the concept of 'celebrity' is influencing all of us, especially artists and writers.

But as to fiction, let's leave the last words to Jay McGill (a nom de plume used by Duncan Bush) in the first issue of the *Amsterdam Review*:

> There's an overwhelming sense that hype is the only thing concealing a drab and cautious conservatism at the heart of mainstream British publishing.

> The old-fashioned idea of investing in a good writer with small initial sales as seed-corn for the future – or as a loss-leader in firms with a strong commercial list – was sacrificed to the idea of moving books quickly, preferably ones with glossy paper and bright colours . . . An unmistakable sign of this is the way 'personalities' (aka 'celebrities') now dominate publishers' lists. (Bush, 2004d)

Did Bush consider himself a victim of such conservatism? Undoubtedly. That policy has made 'non-persons' of many writers who promised and still promise much. Duncan Bush (in McGill's words) believed that: '*good writers, whether novelists or poets, don't repeat or imitate themselves. What characterizes original talent is a determination not only to make different choices from their contemporaries but write books which are different even from their own*' (Bush, 2004d). I believe *The Genre of Silence* to be a more ambitious but very different volume than the much-lauded *The Noise of Time*, by Julian Barnes, a novel of 2016 which deals with Dmitri Shostakovich, the Russian composer who had to endure Stalinism. We should note that 'the noise of time' was the title of Osip Mandelstam's 'autobiographical sketches'.

'For Osip Emilievich Mandelstam' is one of *The Genre of Silence*'s 'poems from the Stalin Years'. It was composed by Victor Bal, in reality Duncan Bush himself. Indeed, the image of a caged bird, in this case a goldfinch, figures on artist John Selway's original cover for the first Poetry Wales Press (Seren Books) edition:

> Safer, you thought, in days
> like these, to live a bird
> than as a man,
> pretending to forget that
> cagebirds sing, and can be heard.
>
> (1988b)

Mandelstam's own goldfinch poem(s) dates from December 1936, written whilst 'in internal exile'. He died in imprisonment in winter 1938, undergoing hard labour for 'counter-revolutionary activities'.

What Duncan Bush thought of Barnes's *The Noise of Time* ('A great novel, Barnes's masterpiece' (Preston, 2016)), I am unsure. But he was sometimes stung into satire when he considered authors who achieved undeserved success. His *Now All the Rage* (2007) attests to this. The creative writing industry creates many such, and it seemed to appal him, despite his sometimes partaking himself of its occasional largesse. Thus poems such as 'Poetess' and 'Learning to Write: a Tutorial' appeared in his poetry collection *Midway* (1997). These are not his best work, yet can entertain at least those who have themselves worked in the industry.

Duncan Bush on his Facebook site (occasionally used from 2013 to 2016), responded on 1 October, 2014, to my comments on *The Genre of Silence* and the *Amsterdam Review* in an initial draft of my submission to *Wales Arts Review* for 'Greatest Welsh Novel': 'I'm grateful for this ... from Robert, who, I fear, knows me too well not to see through many of my authorial ruses and disguises'. For novels of real achievement, the reader should seek out both *The Genre of Silence* and *Glass Shot* (Bush's second novel), paperback or not. Both are utterly unalike. They certainly 'extend fictional forms', as McGill/Bush wrote in the first issue of the *Amsterdam Review* (2004d).

The Genre of Silence was reprinted by Seren in 1995. Its publishers describe it as fitting into a section titled 'Fiction, History, Literary Fiction, Non Fiction'. One section of the book, 'In the Pine Forest', was adapted to become a radio play in 1991. And Bush's work as a playwright is the focus of the next chapter.

Notes

1 *The Complete Works of Isaac Babel* (Norton, 2002), but other collections subsequently: *Red Cavalry and Other Stories* (Penguin Classics, 2005), *Odessa Stories* (Pushkin Press, 2018).

2 See Morson, 'Isaac Babel's Genre of Silence' (2002).

7

Playwright

As a writer, Duncan Bush always enjoyed the fluidity he discovered in differing genres. Thus it is not surprising Bush wrote the following plays, of which only *Sailing to America* has been published; it is therefore the main focus of this chapter.

Theatre plays:
Cocktails for Three (produced Oxford, 1979).
Ends (produced Cardiff, 1980).
Sailing to America (produced Cardiff, 1982).
Journeys (joint winner of the 'Play for Wales' competition).

Radio plays:
In the Pine Forest (adapted from *The Genre of Silence*, 1991).
Are There Still Wolves in Pennsylvania? (adapted from the poem in *Masks*, broadcast 1990).

Television play:
Sailing to America (broadcast 1992).

Sailing to America was the only play noted by Duncan Bush in his list of publications for *Now All the Rage* (2007). However, it is not mentioned in *The Flying Trapeze* (2012), indicating that perhaps it possessed less importance for Bush towards the end of his life.

In 'Screen Life', possibly a fragment of a wider memoir, given to me by Annette Weaver in January 2021, and from which I quote liberally in this work, Bush writes that: 'The first tv programme I recall watching with any regularity were the Sunday night ABC Armchair Theatre plays, which began in 1960. These included an odd, raw, compelling drama called "A Night Out", by an author named Harold Pinter, in which not much happened.' Not much 'happens' in *In the Pine Forest*, a reading of parts of *The Genre of Silence*, Bush's novel in which excellent poems are 'framed' by pieces of prose. But the very subject matter (Stalin's Great Terror) provides all necessary tension without any requirement to state the theme.

Duncan's biography in the Seren plays, *Act One Wales*, containing *Sailing to America*, tells us: 'He [Bush] is becoming more involved in writing drama for the stage and screen, including a recent BBC documentary about the origins and history of cinema in Wales and a commissioned TV play' (Clark, 1997). And it continues: 'Written in 1989, *Sailing to America* is set in a stark hospital ward where two very different women, through a lengthy and diverse conversation, discover each other's dreams, disappointments and desires.'[1]

Mentioned in this play is Lavernock, part of the coast near Barry in south Wales, a place of Bush's childhood, and referenced also in his second novel, *Glass Shot* (see chapter 2 in this volume for his memories of travelling there by train).

In *Sailing to America*, similarly to *In the Pine Forest*, not much happens. Towards the play's end, Evelyn says to Josie, talking about hospital visiting: 'But it was like it was a happy bus. Not sad. Like they were all going down Lavernock or Barry Island in a Whitsun treat. Like in the old charabancs' (Bush, 1997b). As *Sailing to America* is set in a 'terminal ward', and knowing Bush's concerns with Russian literature, especially the period up to and including the Great Purge or the Great Terror, the subject of *The Genre of Silence*, the author was obviously aware of Solzhenitsyn's *Cancer Ward*. This novel was gradually composed until 1966, then partially published in samizdat form, until it was leaked or smuggled and translated in sections (first English edition 1968).

Sailing to America owes more to Harold Pinter than Solzhenitsyn, but is fascinating because it contains familiar Bush images and tropes. Amongst these are 'Hollywood' and named actors, such as Hedy Lamarr and Paul Muni. (There is Pinteresque discussion as to whether Paul Muni actually appeared in the film *Casablanca*.) Other stars referenced include Errol Flynn, William Holden and Ingmar Bergman. Bush never used names without good reason. These Hollywood icons have significance. Paul Muni also features in *Masks* (1994), in 'A.I.D.S. (The Movie)', and in the part of Pasteur in the 'monochrome Lives of the Great Scientists' in the same poem.

America, then, seems the ultimate destination for both women in this play, as their desultory conversation in the terminal ward appears to make clear. We should note M. Wynn Thomas's assertion in *Corresponding Cultures* that 'America is for Duncan Bush, the wannabe internationalist, what Abercuawg is for the confirmed nationalist R. S. Thomas' (1999, p. 247).

The images used by the two characters in *Sailing to America* are plucked from afternoon television films, which is typical of Duncan Bush. Films, and where and how they are viewed, are vital to his writing. And, as he writes in the unpublished memoir 'Screen Life': 'The films I loved when I was a child, I admire fifty years later.'

Josie, mid-play, describes a noise she hears:

> It's like you're going somewhere on a ship. The noise of the engine room. (pause) Sometimes even when I'm asleep I hear it. (pause) I can feel the movement under me. The ocean. And then I know it is a ship. And it's taking me somewhere. It's like the whole hospital, all those wings and floors lit up, and me on my bed in it, is steaming off into the dark. Like a big transatlantic liner sailing off to America. (pause) And I think, this is it. I've always wanted to see America. (pause) And I know this is a trip I won't wake up on. (Bush, 1997b)

Then, a little later, Evelyn qualifies Josie's vision of Hollywood and its stars with:

> And you know that's not really the sea behind them. And they're not really on the deck of a ship. It's just a bit of rail, with some kind of film on a screen, or whatever it is they use, to show that twinkly shimmery look of the sea;

> (pause) it's like in the South Seas or somewhere. You know, with the moon on it, and the night so clear. (pause) And you can see it's not real. It's just a background. But it always used to make me think. (Bush, 1997b)

What Evelyn is describing is a 'glass shot'. Here is Ephraim Katz's statement, in the *International Film Encyclopedia* (1982), quoted at the beginning of Bush's novel, *Glass Shot*, as to what an actual 'glass shot' is:

> A shot obtained through a glass plate on which part of the scene has been painted. The painting on the glass is photographed along with the action seen through the clear portion of the glass, providing the illusion of a complete setting. This Special Effect can be used to simulate elaborate locations without the need to construct expensive sets. (Bush, 1991)

Josie believes in the 'ship' she hears, even if it is in a dream. Evelyn points out what is actually happening. This dramatic scene might be quoted to critics of Duncan Bush's second novel.

Both women have loved the experience of watching films. Evelyn is especially clear:

> During the war everything was dark at night . . . Because of the blackout. But afterwards, everything had that moonlit sort of sheen. Life was so drab by daylight. Everything was on ration. Except for the pics. Your life only started at night, in the queue to those films. (Bush, 1997b)

What Seren, the publishers of the play, recall most vividly is the length of Evelyn's final speech (Mick Felton, verbal communication, March 2023). I agree, and believe this a dramatic flaw. I note that in his earliest dramatic writing, in Oxford, Bush was both actor and possibly director, as well as author.

Yet, for any restaging of *Sailing to America*, this might be rectified. I would be happy to see it performed again, understanding that issues such as mixed marriages and resulting mixed-race children, referenced in the play, are an unremarkable part of ordinary life, but possibly not during the immediate post-Second World War years.

The play's location, explicitly around the Moorland Road (Splott) area of Cardiff, gives it a secure grounding, as do the references to Shirley Bassey. I also note Stew Boyle's mixed race heritage (Maltese and Irish) in *Glass Shot*.

Evelyn's long final speech faces facts. She describes the last make-up applied to patients for two reasons – to ensure they are, both when alive and when dead, more 'presentable'. I feel the speech could have been broken up with more interjections from Josie, such as the earlier, 'Like, what did I ever do to anyone?'

As to the bus that arrives and departs:

> But nobody goes from here. Not on the bus. (pause) But sometimes I think I will. As if it's been coming here and waiting just for me, all this time. (pause) And that's what it'll be like. Not like an ambulance, with those horrible black windows, or a big slow hearse. But on that orange bus. So you can look at the houses, parks. And sit. With people. (Bush, 1997b)

Of course, 'that orange bus' is an accurate but not indispensable Cardiff allusion; Cardiff City Council noted:

> The orange buses were first introduced in August 1972 and were used until the turn of the millennium. From May 2016 Cardiff buses were repainted in the livery which was familiar to so many to celebrate 30 years since [Cardiff Bus] took over as a council-owned arms-length bus firm. (*Wales Online*, 2016)

Like much of his other writing, *Sailing to America* draws on Bush's interests in experimenting with different genres. The next chapter discusses his second novel, *Glass Shot*, also set in Cardiff, and, significantly, more rural Wales.

Note

1 While *Act One Wales* states that *Sailing for America* was written in 1989, Pagnoulle (1995), refers to a 1982 production of the play in Cardiff.

8

Glass Shot (1991)

Bush's second novel, *Glass Shot*, is a depiction of a male character failing to come to terms with rejection by his wife and thus the loss of his two children. At the same time the reader becomes aware that this man is a resentful stalker and a clear danger to women. *Glass Shot* is set in Cardiff and south Wales in 1984 and 1985, the time of the UK miners' strike.

I recall talking incessantly to several writers about the strike, especially John Tripp, Duncan Bush and Nigel Jenkins. Our part of the M4 motorway – between Swansea and Newport – was central to miners, police, 'scab coal' and picketing activity. Bush was at this time commuting from Ynyswen in the north of the Swansea and Neath valleys to Newport, sometimes a difficult journey, especially when, as Annette Weaver informed me, his car broke down.

Perhaps this incident could be the basis for the scene in *Glass Shot* when the main character, Stew Boyle, remarks on the constant lorry traffic on the motorway: 'something fucking scary about so many lorries travelling so close together . . . It's like we're in a state of war' (Bush, 1991). The *Glass Shot* part of Wales outside Cardiff was very badly affected by coalmine closure. Today, only drift mining in Aberpergwm continues, while the huge opencast site extension near Merthyr Tydfil (Ffos y Fran), the last in Wales, closed in 2023.

Places that attracted criticism and dismissal by Stew Boyle (and thus, seemingly – to some – by Duncan Bush) in this area probably included Onllwyn, Banwen, Cwmgwrach, Seven Sisters, Resolfen, Rhigos, Neath and Glynneath. In 1984 Duncan Bush and Annette

Weaver had purchased their first home, Godre Waun Oleu, in Ynyswen, on the northern tip of the coalfield and not significantly different from these other places.

As previous chapters have shown, the miners' strike infuses most of Duncan Bush's writing at this time, especially *Glass Shot* (1991), *Salt* (1986) and *Black Faces, Red Mouths* (1985), a pamphlet used again in *The Hook* (1997).

When I read *Glass Shot* first, I was surprised by Stew (Stoo) Boyle's cowboy outfit, worn in the Locomotive pub. Reread again and again, thirty years later it seems likely his drinking companion, Colin, is mocking him for his 'western' cowboy clothes. Viewed from today, Boyle's carefully assembled outfit gives him the cultural impact of a bad tribute band: sad, almost surreal.

Duncan Bush is one of the 'younger' writers dealt with in M. Wynn Thomas's *Corresponding Cultures*, in the chapter 'Wales's American Dreams'. Thomas quotes the character 'Mother' in Ed Thomas's *House of America*:

> You don't have to go to the Wild West to find America; they've got a Wild West up the valley – you can go there and be a cowboy for a day. You can dress in your cowboy outfit, have a drink in the saloon, and they've got Country and Western singers every Friday and Saturday night . . . The bloke who told me is a cowboy, he thinks he's a cowboy anyway. (1999)

House of America is one of *Three Plays* published by Seren in 1994. We should be aware that *Glass Shot* first appeared in 1991, so it may have influenced the play.

Glass Shot is much more than the advertised claim, 'psychological thriller' (on the cover of the 1993 paperback edition). Unpleasantly relentless, as Margaret Minhinnick, fellow reader, insists, its sinister undertones gradually become terrifying. This is surely what the author craved – because Bush wishes to create terror. What he does not aspire to is explicit horror. And the difference between terror and horror is for the reader to decide.

I believe Stew Boyle was initially considered by Duncan Bush when he wrote 'Brigitte Bardot in Grangetown', a poem first collected in *Masks* (1994) but published earlier, as 'Bardot in Grangetown', in *Poetry Wales* (Bush, 1988a). In this poem, the writer creates a scene, 'off Ferry Road, the toilet of a garage', and especially 'out where they eat', an area replete with typical Bushian imagery of particular tools, including 'the clenched vice'. It is also decorated with photographs of Brigitte Bardot and footballer Ian Rush cut from newspapers, especially by 'a six-month Government trainee':

> a bit simple, they all thought.
> *A headbanger*

Might such a young man grow up to be Stew Boyle?

> He left the other week,
>
> the trainee. He didn't finish, he never even came
> back for his tools
>
> (1988a)

A failure similar to Boyle's.

Jane Aaron and M. Wynn Thomas (2003), in the chapter 'Pulling You Through Changes: Welsh Writing in English Before, During and After Two Referenda', single out 'Bardot in Grangetown': 'where the sympathetic identification with a mentally "simple" trainee mechanic, is in part, Bush's expression of imaginative solidarity with the whole underclass of workers he so memorably recorded in 'Navvies' and other poems in *Salt*'. And I would add, yes, 'sympathetic identification' and 'imaginative solidarity' is what good writers are capable of, because it provides them with ideas for their own work. Such cross-fertilisation is vital.

Richard Poole, in his essay 'Duncan Bush's Personae', states that Stew Boyle 'represents a perfectly natural development, and shows [Bush] exploring for the first time, provocatively and excitingly, an unsympathetic persona' (1992b).

For a man in his mid-thirties, Boyle's dream of the USA is dangerously romantic. He is a map-reader who knows the capitals of US states, such as Bismarck, North Dakota: 'You can spend hours over a map, it's better than a good book, better than even going to the place' (Bush, 1991). He also mourns the 'loss' of English county names, such as Rutland and Huntingdonshire, after local government restructuring in 1974, yet seems oblivious to the losses and changes closer to home in Welsh county restructuring. Duncan Bush's new home village was once in Brecknockshire. After 1974 this became Powys. Such ignorance is intentional on Bush's part. Boyle is a type of Cardiffian the novelist well understood, seemingly anti-Welsh language, as the poet was sometimes and mistakenly considered to be.

In the EU referendum, Cardiff voted to remain. But Boyle surely would not have (if he even bothered to vote). His politics are infantile and paranoiac. 'It's true what I say; every day they're taking more and more away from us so we can't recognize ourselves in things any more'. This is very similar to the campaign waged by those who sought to take the UK out of the European Union, by 'taking it back'.

In the desperation of the final chapters, Boyle describes his politics: 'I'm no "Marxist". There'll be no "re-education" for those bastards. All there'll be for them is a quicklime grave. My kind of Marxist is more like Pol Pot. Like he said: Owning a typewriter even is a sin'.

Once outside Cardiff, Boyle, on his way to his ex-wife's new home in south Breconshire (Powys), soon finds himself alienated. It's not only the coal-carrying and intimidatory lorries on the M4, but once west and north of Neath, where Boyle purchases his camping gear for sleeping out, even the landscape is at first threatening, then dreamlike.

> And on a clear day like it is again today it's like it must be Wyoming, or Montana, like a background you'd see in a film. Or some Shangri-La, another mountain land painted on glass . . . Because it's suddenly like you're not in Wales any more. You're in America.

But Wales poses problems. For Boyle, what appear derelict mining villages is one thing and a subject for scorn and belittlement, but the Welsh language itself is an inexplicable linguistic barrier, and quite another. His own country makes him feel foreign. As he is. Or as he deliberately makes himself, with pointless and aggressive bravado. At the very end of the novel, ex-wife Carol wonders at his surprise at having been spotted on a spying mission in the hills above her house. She points out that he had parked his blue Thunderbird automobile on a narrow mountain road. Her own community had informed her of this intrusive vehicle. Boyle's own community, whether at the tyre-fitting garage or in the pub, considers him alien, unreliable and physically menacing. (Boyle is finally dismissed from work for unexplained absenteeism – his time given over to stalking and spying.)

But not only does Wales resemble a landscape seen through a painted 'glass shot', Boyle believes he enters a differently conscious state when engaged on his stalking of women: whether it's of Rusty (a client from the garage), a sixth-former in a suburb of north Cardiff, other unnamed women, or his ex-wife:

> it's as if I can stop my heartbeat and go transparent. Like when that girl's flatmate came back and went into that other room and stood there in the doorway with her back to me and screamed and screamed and I walked across the lit room behind her and through the door she had just opened, into the hall of the flat; and then into the corridor and away through the out door that she's just closed and locked and put the safety-chain on as well.

Undoubtedly, Duncan Bush wishes his reader to suppose that Stew Boyle is a psychopathic murderer. Boyle loves to watch and follow his victims and invade their most private space when they are least expecting it. Thus Rusty, whom Boyle has met in the garage when changing her tyre, is appalled when she discovers this intruder in her apartment after she returns from her Spanish holiday, Boyle having copied her house keys he has already stolen.

Of his stalking and burgling missions, he says: 'I try never to leave without some Souvenir of some kind.' And what should the reader understand by that capital 'S'? 'A lock of hair. A bra. A scarf I used.' Used? Even a diaphragm. 'Don't worry', he says, to one victim. 'You won't be needing this now for a while'.

Boyle is addicted to the smells of his victims. There is a litany of what he loves to sniff, to breathe in, conveyed to the reader via his particularising descriptive ability, which is one of the most powerful aspects of Bush's writing:

> I lift the flap of the handbag and inhale again a faint clean feminine cosmetic smell . . .
>
> The handbag is like a small satchel in design. Good leather. Hardwearing, serviceable. Space and Style for the modern working Miss. Mushroom, they call it; this greyish beige. . . .
>
> a one-piece swimming costume: black, with a green flash at the hip . . .
>
> jeans, best of all, to put your nose delicately just there where the double-stitching runs back under her . . .
>
> Everything I touch she has touched . . . I take out the yellow plastic comb, and there is a single brown hair caught in the teeth. (It is enough to conjure with.) And then I find her mirror. A small oblong hand-mirror bordered with imitation tortoiseshell. (1991)

Boyle masturbates on to the mirror, leaving 'barely a smear, the smallest smudge, like a sample on a slide. Unidentifiable except under a microscope. So small she'll never know it's there. But there. Every time she checks her face'. This occurs in the underground toilets at Hayes Island in Cardiff city centre: 'The cavelike trickle of green Victorian plumbing . . . That faint, tidal whiff of Lavernock beach and seaweeded rocks and the old rusty sewage pipe'.

Perhaps Boyle is not impotent, but his pathological state is made clear here. In his interview with Richard Poole Bush notes:

> it's a clinically recognized fact . . . psychopaths – which is something you might feel Stew Boyle to be – often have markedly developed intelligence,

frequently in verbal ways . . . Finally it should be unnecessary to point out that Glass Shot is a novel, not a testimony taken from a real person.

The author also states: 'A lot of people have told me they find my novel, Glass Shot, disturbing. But on a second reading . . . find it very funny. Can it be both?' (Poole, 1992a).

Bush is here responding to critics (early readers of the novel, but later those on social media), who claim Boyle, a working-class tyre-fitter/mechanic, has an unrealistic vocabulary. For instance, this remark by 'Peter' on the Goodreads website:

> When a prize-winning Welsh poet unexpectedly writes a crime novel, the result should be something well beyond the ordinary – a feast of language at the very least.
>
> Ah well. The first-person narrator is a divorced tyre-fitter from Cardiff who has a hang-up about women in general and his ex-wife in particular coupled with some ill-formed fantasies about America (he hangs around in a cowboy shirt and a 1957 Thunderbird). Maybe Duncan Bush thought that writing about Cardiff low-lifes was so easy you just didn't have to bother – have the narrator say fucking this and fucking that, have him leer at women from time to time, and that should do it. Don't bother listening to how people talk. Don't bother that we are supposed to be in South Wales. (2018)

Bush, who always possessed a distinctive north Llandaff accent, very different from other 'South Wales' accents, if he had read this, would surely have shaken his head here. 'Peter' continues:

> Don't bother that your tyre-fitter keeps forgetting who he's supposed to be and starts telling us about the 'coup de foudre' of seeing a girl he fancies, or how much he admires a cinematic shot of the mansard roofs of Paris, or starting a sentence 'It's like that guy Wittgenstein said . . .' (which is where I finally gave up).

Although this remark was made after Bush's death, I can imagine his reaction to that 'who he's supposed to be'.

But this also from 'Math' at the same source. *Glass Shot* is:

> Crime Noir at its best. Beautifully written, suspenseful, and a brilliant exploration of 80's Britain, Consumerism, Globalization and Centre-periphery conflicts. Seen through the perspective of an unreliable narrator of colossal proportions. This book is a forgotten crime noir classic, and I encourage you to read it. Duncan Bush, better known for his poetry, is an excellent writer. Highly recommended. (Goodreads, 2015)

Stew Boyle fantasises about what Rusty (the first 'victim' the reader is aware of) is feeling and thinking, denying the evidence of his own eyes and her behaviour. 'Something she hadn't realized or quite put together before. But she's realized it now and it's given her a new strength; the quiet strength to wait, to be patient' (Bush, 1991). Strength? The strength to understand that the man Rusty is with is 'not the one'. Because Stew Boyle is 'the one', and Stew Boyle is only yards away on a seat close by in the Hayes Island snack bar in central Cardiff. As he will be five minutes later at the bar in Bernie's Bistro in Charles Street, stealing the handbag which she's left on her stool, containing air tickets to Spain. And as he contemplates his victims, Boyle imagines them thinking: 'Next time our eyes will meet for ever, and they'll love me' (1991). In fact, Boyle's life is dominated by masturbatory, self-pitying dreams, a theme which links this novel with the much later *Now All the Rage* (2007).

Duncan Bush, in an unpublished autobiographical fragment, describes a childhood game of hide-and-seek in the home of his friend Ceri. Duncan hides in a large wicker clothes basket for dirty washing:

> I don't know how long I'm in hiding, tense, waiting, careful not to make the wicker creak: but it's not the playmate who's looking for me who finally comes into the bedroom but Ceri's mother. I crouch there in the basket, knowing only not to make a sound. What I'm certain of is that she undresses, or perhaps changes an item of clothing, but I'm not sure if I see this through the wicker or can tell from the noises she makes. What I do remember is the feeling of guilt and an instinct for self-denunciation which

> makes me want to fling back the lid, stand up in the basket and reveal my presence, like a triton surging up out of a wave. But I also know that this will terrify her, and so master the compulsion and wait fearfully, without giving myself away.

The fragment continues:

> This incident arouses a strong erotic connotation for me now that I'm not sure it had at the time. How old was I? Ten? Eleven? Certainly I must have been small enough to climb into a washing-basket (but then, doesn't the gargantuan Falstaff find his way into one too?) In fact many of the details of what happened are unclear to memory, and the temptation is, again, to permit myself to see and understand more now, through the fictionalizing imagination, than I did then – to depict myself, that is, with one eye pressed to a gap in the weave of the wicker while a mature married woman takes off various articles of clothing. Yet the tension I recall is as intense as that of eroticism, and it's tempting to speculate that the event had some formative significance – as if, say, it was in the role of voyeur that I was first confronted with the mystery of sexual intimacy.

This was almost certainly written after Bush had published *Glass Shot* and his 'fictionalizing imagination' created Stew Boyle, who steals and hides from, stalks, observes, follows, terrifies and possibly murders women.[1]

Boyle's very last words to, or about, his ex-wife and her partner, ending chapter 14, are an incoherent listing of expletives, fragments of popular songs, a flood of images from paintings and 'corny tableaus', the worst words he is capable of uttering, and which prove his dangerous infantilism, 'before I smash my way in'.

But chapter 8 of *Glass Shot* is distinctive, a key change from Stew Boyle's rebarbative effing and blinding. In this chapter, we are no longer inside Boyle's head but in Rusty's, who it seems, has taken advantage of the return of her air tickets to Spain and is there for a week. Other characters appear in this section, and once more we have beach scenes in south Europe, as described by Duncan Bush in *Aquarium*. This is another link between the poet and the novelist.

Chapter 8 might exist separately as a short story, although there is no evidence it did. Rusty seems to view her hotel and beach through early morning mist. Nothing is clear, yet the chapter culminates with Rusty masturbating Francisco, a chef she has been introduced to, and who reminds her of 'a guy whose name I never even knew . . . Someone who changed a tyre on my car once'. Only here at the chapter's conclusion do we acknowledge links between Boyle and Francisco. The chef's hair is black 'like an Apache' – exactly as Boyle is described. (Perhaps Francisco is a different version of Boyle? A more benign, even sexually passive incarnation?) In the novel, Stew Boyle has an Irish father and Maltese mother. He is racially distinctive, as many dockland people from Cardiff proudly are, and draws attention to these differences.

But undoubtedly Bush very much wants his reader to imagine the worst about Boyle. For instance: 'It's a terrible thing to say. But I'm glad [my mother's] dead. I'm glad she is. I'm glad she won't ever find out now about me and those things I do'. Those things? Keeping albums and dossiers on various women. (Do we link Boyle here with the government trainee and his pictures of Brigitte Bardot?) Stalking women. Burgling those women's homes. Tying them up. Terrifying them. Brandishing knives around those women. Bush allows the reader to decide whether he murders the women he stalks, but it would be ridiculous to suggest, given the deliberate clues and their implications left by the author, that he does not.

It is surely pertinent that amongst Bush's unpublished papers is an essay on the importance he discovered in 'scrapbooks'. He writes:

> Many things invite speculation, but few conclusively reward it. A scrapbook was a publicly-resourced archive of aspects of the inner-world of the individual compiling it . . . It's truer to speak of the past as a vast, cluttered landfill site, most of which is buried and therefore invisible . . . If I were to discover my old scrapbooks . . . tomorrow, they'd probably mystify me as much as if they'd been compiled by a stranger . . . They were a form of diary, but one that forgetfulness will have translated into unbreakable code.

However, the scrapbooks and dossiers kept by Boyle would require many years until that code was 'unbreakable'.

The reviewer S. T. Dauncey writes:

> *Glass Shot* does succeed in a number of ways, including the way it illustrates the relationship between sex and fantasy; its successful depiction of working-class life and psychological obsession. Bush paints what appears to be a more realistic portrait of a sexual psychopath then novels such as Brett Easton Ellis' pornographic 'American Psycho'. Bush's book offers a null hypothesis: the violent and sexual content a reflection of a realistic character who is warped. Easton Ellis uses sex and violence in a misogynistic, titillating way. Comparisons seem more apt with John Fowles' *The Collector*, whose central character's psychological makeup is similar to Stew Boyle's. (1992)

Ian Gregson has written about Duncan Bush in a letter titled 'Transplanted (Duncan) Bush' that appeared in *Poetry Wales*.

> The self-conscious constructing of Stew Boyle, his authorial stewing and boiling, has a potent political effect – it suggests that his violence is only an unusually extreme product of patriarchy and capitalism. A major achievement of Glass Shot is its defamiliarised exploration of masculinity. The defamiliarising is crucial because masculinity presents itself as the norm, presents its perspective as common sense, its values are universal – the normalizing of masculinity is the most potent weapon – ideological weapon – of patriarchy. (2005)

Throughout the last chapters, Boyle tells us about his head and muscle aches and the anger he feels about how his own life has developed. This actual pain might be part of a psychotic state, based on paranoia, which he enters during his preparations for stalking or burglary. Relief comes when he's engaged on these activities – when his heart rate is stilled and he feels 'transparent'. 'I never meant to, but sometimes you can hardly stop yourself. You don't realize how much tension and rage there is in you when that ticking in your head is all you hear'. And 'Me, I'm the blackest densest object in this landscape. I'm as black and dense as a planet compressed to no bigger than an orange, though it weighs the earth'. Consider that 'clenched vice' again. Yet occasionally the red mists clear from Boyle's eyes during the novel's conclusion, and he sees clearly: 'They don't understand that some things are only pictures [he says of his infant daughter, Mandy]: they think they can have everything they see'. Once again here is Bush's belief that our own fixations with images are proof of our inability to understand the nature of reality. Thus we tear pages out of books, as does Mandy, believing the pictures are the same as the things the pictures portray.

Gradually, a picture of Stew Boyle becomes lodged in the reader's mind. He is a clever and obsessive man, doomed by his own ruthlessness. Boyle is particularly dismissive of 'educated' women, such as Carol, his ex-wife: 'Because anyone who's been around the bitches long enough, let alone been married to one, knows better than to think that any of them is as innocent as they like to make out'.

In the penultimate chapter, Carol's new partner calls her into the adjoining room to see what's on TV. The reader thinks it must be to learn about Stew Boyle, who surely by now has made a police visit to Carol's home imperative. Yet it's to watch televised coverage of the police action against the Orgreave picketers during the miners' strike: 'One man was almost being carried. The nearside of his face was jagged with runnels of blood'. For that moment, Boyle, Carol and partner seem united in condemnation. Yet there might be some kind of final understanding for Boyle. As he contemplates his own life and that of his wife, the analogy for Duncan Bush is typically filmic, or to use an unusual word Bush employs in other similar contexts, 'irreal'. 'I suppose the trouble with my wife and me was we were trying to live in different movies'. And in the interview conducted with Bush in *Poetry Wales*, Richard Poole asked: 'One reviewer declared himself left wondering "where the deciding line is between serious fiction and the porn market". Does this sort of comment make you want to bang your head on the wall?' To which Bush replied: 'Not in the least. In a case like that, the only head that wants banging is the reviewer's' (Poole, 1992a). Unfortunately, Mandarin, the 1993 paperback publisher of *Glass Shot*, misunderstands the main character.

This is from the back cover: 'Stew Boyle is a Welsh yob, a 36-year-old divorced slob garage mechanic vegetating in the valleys.' *Yob* and *slob* and *valleys* in the first sixteen words.

In his biographical note in *Poetry Wales* Duncan Bush 'is currently working on a film version of his novel, *Glass Shot*' (1998). But, as film treatments of modern novels are glacially slow, this yet might happen. Finally, Stephen Knight, in his essay 'A New Enormous Music: Industrial Fiction in Wales', writes:

> more materialistic and more clearly a reversal of collier heroics is Duncan Bush's *Glass Shot* (1991), a novel that can be described variously as urban realism, dark romance and an ultra-modern thriller. It certainly makes use of some of the forms of the criminal-focused psycho-thriller, but it is also conscious of its position as a negative reflex of industrial fiction. The anti-hero is a strong-willed, strong-bodied young man who can only find trivial manual work as a tyre-fitter. His derailed energies flow over into violence and malice, and in a final scene as he roars around south Wales in his large car, he passes a pit where some of the miners, some of the last left now, are on strike. But his glance at them is distant; the connection between male vigour and industrial work has been broken, to the detriment of both. (2003)

This is a valid reading, yet many readers might react to *Glass Shot* in a different way: with a mixture of fear, terror and disgust, as Rusty does when she discovers Boyle inside her apartment.

And it is typical of Duncan Bush's cinematic imagination, that he describes Stew Boyle's escape from Bernie's Bistro, after he has stolen Rusty's handbag, thus:

> I am not actually running. But it is with a visible shudder, as if still expecting a rifle shot behind me and a bullet exactly midway between the shoulder blades, that I turn into Queen Street with my stark black shadow now ahead of me, vacating the bright, abruptly vacant pavement of Charles Street. I am gone from their sight almost in the instant of their eyes' habituation to the sunlight out of doors, so that I leave behind only a glimpse – or even an after-image lingering against the empty perspective of the paving-stones, like in the last frame of a cartoon-strip or a photograph taken a split second too late.

In 2008, Duncan's elder brother, Allan Bush, a retired building surveyor, published his first novel with Seren, Duncan's Welsh publisher. The company's description states: '*Last Bird Singing* is an extraordinary and stunning evocation of one man's inner life, dark, haunting and bitterly true. The walls, pubs and streets of Wales' capital city loom through the blackness of an intense brilliantly realised story of loneliness and loss' (Anon., 2008). The book won the fiction category of the Glen Dimplex New Writers Awards 2008. Academic reviewer Dai Smith has written:

> To be sucked into the slipstream of this ice-cold odyssey through Cardiff past and present is to confront a brute reality which Allan Bush creates in prose as clear and iridescent as oil-slicked puddles on a city street. No one, but no one, has ever written about Cardiff's deep reality like Bush does: attempts at Noir pale into insignificance before its deep and disturbing blackness of vision. (2008)

Readers may decide for themselves whether Dai Smith has *Glass Shot* in mind here. Either way, it would be seventeen years before Duncan Bush published another novel.

The last three chapters have described Duncan's experiments with writing in different genres in the late 1980s and early 1990s, but poetry was always central in his work, and the next chapter focuses on two collections published during the 1990s.

Note

1 This previously unknown autobiographical fragment was read by myself at the Association of Welsh Writers conference, Gregynog, May 2024.

9

Masks (1994) and *Midway* (1997)

In a long (but not long enough) publishing career, Duncan Bush's best poems are concentrated in the Seren collections *Masks* (1994) and *Midway* (1997), together with his first Seren novel, *The Genre of Silence* (1988), which was discussed in chapter 6. Gradually, his poetic output slowed.

Masks boasts 'Living in Real Times (Summer 1993)', a long-lined, maybe messy mix of cricket and unspecified conflict – 'Sarajevo? Mostar? Vukovar?' – glimpsed on multi-screens in Queen Street, Cardiff, Bush considering 'the instant replay and the freezeframe', his eye attuned 'to the destined fact, knowing there's no way out' (1994a). For Bush, the plethora of screens means we are now complicit in whatever is being televised, whether cricket, earthquake or warfare. We cannot fail to take part, even momentarily, as in 'Living in Real Times'. The screens are Orwellian.

'The Sunday the Power Went Off', is similarly powerful, not merely for its depiction of the shocked reaction it provokes in the Bush household, but because it states what many of us feel, brought up on concepts of atomic warfare and environmental collapse. Surely, all modern writing occurs within these shadows and has done for many years. Thus, here we find 'Just a Few Things Daddy Knows about Ice' and 'After Chernobyl'. This, after all, is the poet who contributed liberally to an anthology for the anti-apartheid movement:

    that
first faint flash I know

may any time come before a roar
as of wind and of whirlwind,
finding me sitting

knowing instantly under clear air this wasn't lightning, seeing
wife, sons, sunlight suddenly

reversed, as in a negative

'The Sunday the Power Went Off' (1994a)

Almost biblical language here, and the reader might quote back, 'Out of the south cometh the whirlwind; and cold out of the north' (Job 37: 9). This is the poet comfortably at home, yet envisioning nuclear oblivion.

Always Bush was attracted to film, screens and their paraphernalia. But also to atlases. This is clear in *Glass Shot*, as well as throughout the poems. 'Coming Back', from *Masks*, gives a nod to Baudelaire, but it's Bush's (rather disappointing?) Cardiff that insists:

Every time you come back
It's shrunk again

while 'Part 3' of the poem would seem to contain its real subject. We learn that 'In the blue grammar-school Oxford atlas':

Oceans were hyacinth,
and mountain ranges rose fawn
through ochre-browns to violet

Yet it's losses the poet mourns. His own, being depicted in his familiar style of using particularities to speak for a wider theme. He feels:

unmanned, suddenly awash
in the unmapped particular, find you
know every kerb and gatepost,

that shaggy hedge of

dusty privet or suburban
laurel, the little striped
snails on the crumbling walling,
a manufacturer's name still

stamped on the old cast-iron
cover of a drain

(1994a)

Critic Christine Pagnoulle (1995) writes about *Masks*:

> Perceptiveness and empathy are equally developed whether his speakers are women or men. It is, for instance, through the farmer's widow and miner's daughter in the short sequence 'Farmer's Widow, Tawe Valley' that he manages to express emotions at the destruction of loved places in a way he would probably have shied away from in his own voice.

This is a tendency in Bush's poetry also drawn attention to by Ian Gregson (2005) – a trait Gregson feels links him to an older 'Anglo-Welsh' sensibility.

The first poem in *Masks*, 'European Capital', has always reminded me of *Glass Shot*. Subtitled 'the dream poem of the South African mercenary', it seems to picture a man almost at the end of a mission. Maybe this 'I' of 'European Capital' has echoes of the almost novel-long soliloquy of *Glass Shot*'s Stew Boyle, especially in the poem's Section 3, 'Café Europa':

Her long red hair dragged
like a bloodied mop across
the bathroom lino, to and fro

Though, admittedly, there is nothing as viciously blatant as this in the novel. But such imagery has occurred from the beginning, as in the 'Hotel Leopold' section:

> After what these good Belgians did
> to her country and its people
>
> can it matter what you or I do with her?

Typically for Bush, 'European Capital' has disconcerting changes of register: Vermeer in the Rijksmuseum; 'a moist vulvo-vaginal sound', and a nativity scene from the 'Rue du Congres' section, the three kings bringing 'guns, uncut heroin and myrrh'. And in the 'Rue de la Loi' section, the 'South African' protagonist feels himself resemble 'Harry Lime' when it dawns on him that, whatever it is, the game's up.

Again, this is Bush's recourse to childhood and later film image memory, whether for prose or poetry. A powerful and demanding piece of writing, this, but possibly too rich in detail. Where does that 'milk-blue Swede masseuse' come from? There are elements of Amsterdam as well as Brussels here, reminding us of what Bush's co-editor of the *Amsterdam Review*, P. C. Evans, says of collaborating with Duncan on their 'new magazine for European literature' (quoted in chapter 11).

It is possible, I find, to compare the 'Hotel Leopold' section with the short story 'Boss', that appeared in *Poets Against Apartheid* in 1986. This also features South Africans:

> I go for
> the black in leopardskin lycra.
> Without the speckled dress, shoes, wig
>
> she is the more leopard, small, round-cropped
> skull, shoulders muscled for speed

The story is also developed with plentiful physical imagery of a woman painting herself a richer black. Or maybe 'black' for the first time. Almost inevitably here, the stories of her 'clients' are 'straight out of the comics; or those old Tarzan films they kept repeating on TV'.

Films are a treasury for the poet, and in 'A.I.D.S. (The Movie)' we have not only 'cultish horror movies from the 'Fifties', but a fond imagining of stars who might appear in a biopic of whoever finds a 'cure' for AIDS. Here Bush is remembering television on 'wet Sunday afternoons in winter', while in 'Late Night Hotel Room with Japanese Transistor Radio', there's harking back to families crouching around, not a television this time but a radio, the BBC Home Service and its 'exotic wavelengths (Kalundborg, Algiers and Hilversum . . .)'. Superb detail, as in 'European Capital'. But perhaps overly crammed.

The collection also contains the understated (and the better for it) 'For the Hawk Fallen', and two other poems made much more of elsewhere in this volume (see chapter 4), the Stalin-era Great Terror-inspired 'Crocuses':

> But word
> went down the heating pipes,
> leaked out through
> even screamproofed walls

and 'Brigitte Bardot in Grangetown' (see chapter 8). I find both seminal in Bush's writings.

In 1995, *Masks* won the Wales Book of the Year award. It was also a Poetry Book Society Recommendation. The volume is dedicated, as so many of Bush's books are, to his family, 'Annette, Joe and Lucas'.

Another volume of poems followed in 1997. The original cover of *Midway* was a gloomy impression of a 1950s film, with the author, in fedora, looking on. And taking it all in. Another fedora-tipping tribute to classic film.

'Rhubarb', in which Bush describes transporting illicitly and planting a rhubarb root in France, is on the face of it, a gardening poem, such as 'Couch Grass', from *The Flying Trapeze*, with a global and personal significance. This, from 'Rhubarb':

Fifty now,
. . .
my senses sharpen too, and each Springtime's
more acute

Because even here, Bush must reveal himself more widely:

I'm no patriot and I'm proud of it.
But it's into language we're born, it's there
we discover the world.

Bush must recognise that he is transplanting himself, and his family, following his wife's career. Embarking on their own 'river of adventure' means an exciting and, yes, satisfying future, he hopes. Look, the poet seems to be saying, at us! The poem continues:

We live here at 330 metres a.s.l. –
over a mountain's height – and face due west
. . . .
where sunset makes it seem we're at an edge
of the world.

The Bushes have become expeditionaries and even pathfinders. 'Shrikes at Jaulny', also in 'The Dark Wood' sequence (*Midway*), gives similar exactitudes of where the new Bush household is actually located. Yes, we've made it. And why not? Is Duncan Bush asking us to follow?

This underlines a good deal of what the autobiographical essay 'Lash LaRue and the River of Adventure', included in *Midway*, depicts – the quiet determination of the schoolboy, on whom the delights of art and literature are dawning, now taught by his father how to eat, of all things, rhubarb, from the poem of the same name:

dabbing
and dabbing it in gritty white sugar
the glands in my jawline watering and

making half-soured faces: how I ate it
as a child from my father's railway line
allotment the day he told me its name.

In the end what language (and I take it the poet means *any* language) demands is determination to chew its bittersweet, no, astringent, cud. Forever.

Daniel G. Williams refers to 'Lash LaRue and the River of Adventure' in *Wales Unchained*: 'While Bush recognizes that the America of his childhood imagination is a myth based on ignorance . . . it is an enabling myth and continues to offer a significant point of orientation for the poet's later writings' (2015). But it's also Bush's reading of W. G. Sebald, as published in the *Amsterdam Review* (see chapter 11), that should be recalled. Bush praises Sebald's 'scrupulous didacticism', having 'raised ontological disgruntlement to an encyclopedic level'. For Bush, Sebald is 'an endlessly observant yet mournful presence, inhabiting or inhabited by some unexpressed grief or guilt' (2005c). As Duncan Bush grew older he found himself drawn to writers such as Sebald and Pavese, who never depended on or were consoled by an American 'myth'.

Midway begins with the suite 'The Fifties', with the memorable and prize-winning (Cardiff International Poetry Competition, 1996) 'Uncle Charlie', and the savage war memories of Uncle Cliff in 'The Song in Our Heart':

the whole
network of uncles; aunts; cousins.
Listening, like all the families in the land,

the great mycelium

Both poems might be said to be based on traditional 'Anglo-Welsh' subject matter, that is, family memories, in the 1950s, very much wartime recalled, about the living and the dead, 'marmoreal and immemorial alike'. 'Old Prosser' and 'Cousin Colin' are also part of the suite 'The Fifties', the latter poem rich with a vocabulary of particularities that today might require its own glossary: Dan Dare, Dennis Compton, G. M. Vauxhall Conference, 'Brylcreemed, patted, silvering quiff'; while:

> Cousin Colin was odder, with
> his 5,000-piece jigsaws and replica fruit.

Such scrumptious detail is now forever surreal.

Adrian Osbourne, on behalf of the Centre for Research into the English Literature and Language of Wales (CREW) at Swansea University, has provided helpful notes on '"Caroline": a County Life', in the 'Provincial Sketches' of *Midway* (confusingly, on the Contents page it is listed as '"Caroline": a Country Life'). I imagine, because of the inverted commas, that the poem contains some factualities. As Adrian Osbourne notes online: it 'takes the focus away from, yet also strangely highlights, the individual at the heart of this narrative' (2020). It is not a flattering portrait of the woman, she being from the first interested in status and a house built of 'brick which is the pale, crumbling red of old money'.

Bush is good about 'money' (see 'What Money is' in the same volume). But Caroline's 'decline' follows a predictable course: 'Twice she fell off her bar-stool at The Flag', while 'The Barman called her "Margaret Rutherford" behind her back'. I would imagine the CREW students pausing at the line 'She reached // a menopause of misery one mild, July night' (1997a). And the death is shocking not because of her manner of suicide but her obviously friendless and abandoned condition. Again from Duncan Bush, here is a poem containing dramatic touches that might have been used in a short story.

'Quotidian' is possibly explicable to a reader of *Glass Shot*. A man returns home after five years to find his bungalow abandoned and despoiled; 'The woman he'd done time for had come downhill too'. Possibly this is another imagining of Stew Boyle, but the language lacks the novel's psychotic propulsion. And the woman? She bears a baby in prison and learns about 'shame'. A strange tale, this, that also might have made a short story. As ever, Bush's poetry teems with dramatic flourishes. But he deems it impossible to develop them all as a reader might wish.

'Gill (1970)' has the poet recalling work as a gasfitter in Anglesey, and perhaps hoping a woman he met years earlier might attend his poetry reading in the Blakeley Hotel, Beaumaris. The poet had been employed to help 'convert the island not to Christianity but North Sea gas'. He paints an ironic portrait of himself:

> Shirt open to the chest, I even sported
> a beachcomber's red bandanna. I think I thought
> . . .
> I was Rimbaud but knew enough to keep the secret
> *from my workmates.*

And of course he understands the romantic dream of a gasfitter, used to working with 'nipples, or olives, or screws', discovered by an ex to be headlining a local literary festival. But the younger Bush was 'another man, on another island'. However, he triumphs in ticking off an 'unusual' word for the first time in one of his poems:

> I sensed, though, the exogamic
> instinct of girls in small Welsh towns
> the evening I strolled across the bar in Holyhead

A clichéd assumption? Also, Bush had wondered if 'Gill' might recall him, again from an image in Bush's imagination, as 'a roughneck in some western'.

It's easy to assume his reference to 'Kuchiouk-Hanem' was to a bath-time beauty product he used when at Gill's home in Amlwch, and not a famous Egyptian (Ghawazee) dancer:

> my first freshwater bath for weeks, and tried out
> your mother's bottled crystals and shampoos.

The comparisons possible to make with Stew Boyle are obvious here, especially in how Boyle describes meeting his wife, then a student, for the first time.

'Down on Britains Farm' is a fifty-long-lined poem which is crammed with detail, too much in fact, to make it comfortable reading. This ends (surprisingly) with a suicide, as does '"Caroline": A County [Country?] Life'. This conclusion might have been better used in a poem of its own. But the poem does contain telling references to 'immaculately-managed scenery', maybe indicating the writer's preference for sculpted environments.

Indeed, there are gloomy overtones to this section, titled 'Provincial Sketches'. The next poem, 'i.m. M. O'N (d.1997)', perhaps could not be anything but:

> How vivid they briefly become when they're dead,
> These individuals we hadn't thought of for years.

Yet Bush recalls: 'We ran half-wild in a gang at the edge of the city', and his lost friend's 'almost fabulous collection of birds' eggs'.

'The Archery Contest (After Virgil, Aeneid, Bk 3)' is a literary 'retelling', 'Eurytion's fatal shaft fletched from a hawk' directing us into 'The Dark Wood', as the last section of the volume is titled, and echoing Dante here. Unique yet familiar intimations now abound. Yet we might have been prepared for this by 'And Suddenly it's Evening', in which 'an old man' sits and ponders his own memories:

> while the dead in
> the churchyard behind him
>
> throw back the turf
> and sit up in the graves as in bed.

Once again, this is Bush's memory linked to imaginative possibility. Here too is the first appearance of his 'smoking couch-grass fire', an image to be expanded in 'Couch Grass' from *The Flying Trapeze* (2012).

As we enter 'The Dark Wood', we learn:

Even
the wind in his neighbour's barley

. . . is telling us
No-one will speak of us after we're dead.

'Midsummer, Night' speaks equally clearly, and with an unmistakable sense of chill:

And life,
which was once vast as the atlas on the shelf,
is closer than your skin, and countable.

And the last poem of all? 'Acherontia Atropos':

A Death's Head hawk moth came
to the privet hedge last night

for nightshade- or potato-flower,
its staples of toxin
. . .
His underwing was eyed,
bloom-scaled damask;
his body furred, fat as a mouse's,
and the skull on his back

was as clear and inevitable
as tomorrow –
a day which in holiday
indolence wasn't decided on yet.

With its blending of intensely local ('For the Hawk Fallen' and 'Coming Back') and international concerns ('European Capital'), *Masks* is Bush's single most impressive collection of poems. It benefits from the inclusion of not only both 'Crocuses' and 'Brigitte Bardot in Grangetown', but also the sequence 'Are There Still Wolves in Pennsylvania?' (which is discussed separately in the next chapter).

Yet *Midway* is Bush's most approachable volume, and possibly his most satisfying, the poet's own intimations of mortality bringing his own life into clearest focus.

10

'Are There Still Wolves in Pennsylvania?' (*Masks* (1994))

Masks describes this as 'a poem sequence in ten parts for two voices' (1994a) and the last part of the collection. It concerns the lives in America of one Vietnam war veteran and his wife, Wesley Rees Ball and Linda Ellen Ball. We are also told that a 'dramatized adaption of this sequence was first broadcast on BBC Radio 3 on October 23rd, 1990' (1994a). For me, yes, it is a radio drama, but also might be described as a novel or a play or a poem.

Duncan Bush has written about his own writing, and is quoted by Christine Pagnoulle (1995):

> Writing is finally like farming. You have a certain area of land of a certain soil type, and all you can hope is to work it all your life.
>
> For me this situation means, among other things, not growing potatoes on the same ground two years running. I write not only poetry but fiction and sometimes even drama, and I need to move between these genres. Occasionally they can be combined, as in my first novel, *The Genre of Silence*, which tells the story of a fictional poet in a dangerous time and includes the poems that outlast him. Or in my collection *Masks* there is a sequence of poems that depict a period of crisis in the relationship between a traumatized former soldier and his wife. When writing my second novel, *Glass Shot*, however, I did not write a poem for over a year. This did not worry me, on the principle already mentioned. It is only leaving one of your fields fallow for a season.

We must remember Duncan Bush had never been a soldier and never known combat as had Wesley Rees Ball, the character, a Vietnam veteran, Bush creates. But then Bush had never been a woman, and yet Linda Ellen Ball plays a significant role in this poem. Does this disqualify Bush from writing 'Are There Sill Wolves in Pennsylvania?' For me, emphatically not. As critic and editor, Richard Poole noted (1992b) that Bush has found himself able to cultivate many personae. Titles of his books include *Masks* and *Glass Shot*, with all that implies.

And Bush was continually drawn to the themes of film and acting, which was especially afforded by his travels in the USA. In his 'Hollywood Wildlife' sequence (uncollected, see chapters 12 and 14), he is attracted to the seamier sides of Los Angeles. This, from 'Vistas of Los Angeles: Night':

> Gulf War Vets bivouac
> In outflow culverts; checking
> The trash-cans like bears.
>
> (2007b)

These 'Gulf War Vets' do not seem dissimilar to Vietnam veterans. Meanwhile, Duncan Bush used the haiku form (roughly, a poem of seventeen syllables, but with Bush a stanza form) a good deal during his later career as a writer (for other examples, see chapters 13 and 14).

Certainly, Wesley Rees Ball can be compared to Stew Boyle from *Glass Shot*, and not merely in the similarity of their names. Both Ball and Boyle complain about various pains. Also, Ball's growing jealousy and suspicion of Linda Ellen, his wife, becomes so profound that he finds himself rummaging through her dirty laundry, a practice that sickens him, and yet, so powerful is his psychosis, he feels compelled to continue it.

But Ball's moods are also anticipated by Linda Ellen, who provides a litany of possible indicators of her own sexual behaviour. This from 'Aphrodisiac' (part 4): 'And / he came up behind / me again, swaying; / and we ended up doing it /for the fourth time / these two days'

(1994a). Because of this, Linda becomes suspicious of Wesley's suddenly increased interest in her.

Yet do his wife's sexual liaisons merely take place in Ball's voyeuristic imagination, fuelling his suspicion? It's notable that Wesley Ball himself compares the male sexual act to the loading and firing of a shotgun. He certainly imagines, in graphic detail, his own suicide with the same weapon. Both Ball and Boyle might be described as fantasists, examples of a 'toxic masculinity' that seeks to exert ever-tighter control over another life, usually a partner's. Such fantasies become self-fulfilling prophecies. And both Ball and Boyle find themselves using shotguns.

In his 1992 interview with Richard Poole, Bush tried to explain the poem (which first appeared in print in this issue):

> In the American psyche the legacy of all this [that is, Vietnam] is still being worked out . . . in booze and dope and anger and psychological pain . . . A thing like this never ends for the people who were there, who saw what happened – many of whom were little more than adolescents at the time. I wanted to show what it felt like to be a participant in that war – or to be married to someone who was – and perhaps, unfortunately, I felt I could only write about it from an American, and not a Vietnamese or Cambodian, point of view. This war still stands as the reversal of Hegel's dictum that history is always written by the victors. (Poole, 1992a)

In the text, Wesley's illness and mental disturbance might be caused by the proximity of power lines to his and Linda Ball's trailer home, or by his terms of duty in Vietnam. Indeed, the immediate environment of the trailer seems brutal, militarised and inhumane, 'all that barbed wire and angle iron outside our windows and stretching twenty miles off in plain view all the way to Harrisburg' (1994a). Linda Ball also complains of poor health: 'migraines and not / sleeping and anxiety and such', which she attributes to the power lines (1994a). Her husband disagrees, stating the power lines carry only 'juice' (1994a).

Wesley Ball is sometimes a hunter, and the image of the dead 'small white-tailed deer not even carrying horns' is powerfully symbolic

(1994a). But Ball himself indicates that hunting might really be an excuse for solitude, even though this provides time to cultivate his suspicions. Hunting is usually a male ritual that Ball has come to distrust and frankly loathe. Yet he considers it an ordeal that must be endured.

In a letter to myself as editor of *Poetry Wales*, critic Ian Gregson noted how Boyle, on the run in Powys, compares himself in *Glass Shot*:

> to those Vietnam veterans living in the forests in Oregon or Washington state; I saw a documentary about them on TV once, they were weird characters; it was like they couldn't cope with everything they'd seen and done out in Vietnam, the Army had turned them into psychos and now they couldn't live in the real world, or the real world wouldn't let them, like with Rambo in *First Blood*. (2005)

It would be absurd to compare Rambo with Rimbaud (or would it?), a poet beloved by Bush. Both men were 'weird' singularities. Yet striking. (Suggested to me by Laura Wainwright is the name 'Ball' shared by Wesley Reece with Private John Ball, from David Jones's *In Parenthesis*.)

Wesley Reece Ball is also made uneasy by the woods, where the hunting takes place. These places seem different, strange, unknowable and to be avoided at any cost. Similarly, in *Glass Shot*, in Stew Boyle's life, Cardiff is familiar and his home. Yet other parts of Wales appear threatening, concealed for some behind the impenetrable Welsh language, by implication, dangerous to all but the Welsh Vietcong.

Fear of the woods is a familiar trope in writing and film-making about America that Bush has gladly adopted, being an admirer of the work of authors such as James Dickey, writer of the novel *Deliverance* (1970). This concerns a group of middle-class male friends who embark on an expedition on a river which is due to be dammed. They meet other men who live in the surrounding forest. This encounter is famously savage. In fact, there is a clear reference to the film of

Deliverance (1972) in 'Dreamback', the final section of 'Are There Still Wolves in Pennsylvania?' Also, surely Bush would have noted Michael Cimino's film *The Deer Hunter* (1978).

In Vietnam, soldiers Ball and Hicks are pondering the corpse of a Vietnamese girl Ball seems to have arbitrarily killed:

> that Tennessee
> hick grin,
>
> the missing tooth –
> Why don't you
> fuck her?
> She's still warm
>
> (1994a)

Here, 'Are There Still Wolves in Pennsylvania?' shares a theme from the poetry of Tony Curtis, a writer also struck by the rituals, and the metaphors these provide, of hunting in the USA. Curtis's sequence *The Deerslayers* (1972) is amongst his most striking poems. Both born in 1946, the two writers were equally energised and appalled by America, which has considerable significance in their writing careers.

In his *Wales Unchained: Literature, Politics and Identity in the American Century*, Daniel G. Williams makes use of *Circus* by Nigel Jenkins (a pamphlet published in 1979 by Swansea Poetry Workshop) as a text intriguing to read alongside 'Are There Still Wolves in Pennsylvania?' Jenkins writes about being 'a roustabout and butcher on a travelling show' in the USA:

> Two shows a day
> seven towns a week.

Bush was surely aware of this poetic sequence before he composed 'Are There Still Wolves in Pennsylvania?' (as I'm sure he was of Tony Curtis's *The Deerslayers* pamphlet from 1972). On the unnumbered pages of *Circus*, Jenkins writes of his work-mates:

Winners, men of action: not for them
the lay-back of car and kids: they've
A war to live up to, decades to kill
. . .
Life
Is the circus, fresh
offensives daily
on their dumbo crew n gook-stupid public.

Meat, smoke and beer on the banks of White River,
The three of them drunk, each with
His scar, the treasured wallet of snaps:
Gook. Gook headless
Gook hanging by his heels.
Gook without body. Gook suspect
Dragged half to death by a truck.
A necklace, another necklace / of gook ears.

'Necklaces of ears', amongst other trophies, has become a familiar image in US literature. Perhaps the most famous (that is, most read) example is found in *Blood Meridian*, by Cormac McCarthy. But this was published first in 1985, six years after Jenkins's *Circus*. 'The man sat holding the necklace in his hands. They wasn't cannibals, he said. They was Apaches. I knowed the man that docked em. Knowed him and rode with him and seen him hung' (McCarthy, 1985). And it is Ball's own reflections on hunting that surely indicate his own acute self-awareness, warped as this might be:

But
what makes me cry
is: what is it
in us that longs so

to bring down
a running thing,
as if to
just see if we can?

(1994a)

And this applies to both a deer and the sixteen-year-old Vietnamese girl 'in black pyjamas', killed by Ball with one 'hell of a shot', who will always now feature in his nightmares.

Stew Boyle's and Wesley Ball's actions are pathological, created by boredom and self-pitying paranoia. In Ball's case his army service in Vietnam must always be borne in mind. The depictions of both men are gripping, but in 'Are There Still Wolves in Pennsylvania?' we also hear Linda Ball's voice, a welcome and worldly feminine counterpoint.

And we should compare Wesley Ball's 'little star-shaped scar . . . scar-shaped star' (1994a) with the scars revealed in 'Miner, Abercynon, 1985' (Bush, 1997c), physical evidence of identity and marks of meaning. For Ball, his scar earned him an escape from warfare; for the Abercynon miner, his blue scars are proof of belonging and class solidarity.

The same might be said of the scars revealed in 'Pneumoconiosis', a Duncan Bush poem, widely published, that appeared first in *Poetry Wales* in 1973 and is available in a full-colour poster by artist Wil Rowlands:

> I'll die with it now.
> It's in me.
> Like my blue scars.
>
> (Bush, 1995b)

In his *Wales Unchained*, Williams writes:

> If Bush identifies with the America of the 'good war' against fascism, the America that seemed to reflect his own multi-ethnic, anti-nationalist, individualism in Cardiff, he is no romanticizer of American realities. 'Are There Still Wolves in Pennsylvania?' forces us, implicitly, to contemplate the dark underbelly of 'American Wales' described with some affection in *Midway*. Bush's writings reveal the sobering truth that to identify with the American dream is also to take some responsibility for the nightmare. (2015)

As to the manner in which the text of 'Are There Still Wolves in Pennsylvania?' is structured, I find many lines, although conveying urgency, inexplicably short, as is the case with many of Bush's later poems. This does not improve the rhythm for reading aloud, or performance. Indeed, the rhythm of later writings, such as the Luxembourg poems (although long-lined) from *The Flying Trapeze* (see chapter 13) appears sometimes prosy. And yet, the poet persisted with these forms.

Again in his interview with Richard Poole, Duncan Bush writes of 'Are There Still Wolves in Pennsylvania?': 'For this sequence the demotic American voice offered me a possibility for a poetic register that could be sufficiently precise and flexible without losing the appearance of the colloquial and everyday' (Poole, 1992a). Bush describes Wesley's character in the same interview:

> Wesley may have gone to college, under the US government's scheme for demobilized personnel. But he's not what one might call an intellectual. He can only live his problems, from the inside – as most problems have to be lived. His wife, Linda, is able to define them, but only for herself, and from the outside. Linda can think and act for herself, and perhaps she's brighter than he is. But she didn't go to college, the name Freud doesn't occur to her, and it's not necessary that it does.
>
> There are hopes for Wesley, though. In the last poem of the sequence at least he perhaps begins to come to terms with the endless loop of his own nightmares. And he doesn't need Freud for that – or a Veteran's Administration counsellor.

In terms of education, *Glass Shot*'s Stew Boyle met Carol, his wife, when she was a student in Bristol, and he a scaffolder. Throughout *Glass Shot* he persists in thinking about her university life in a belittling and dismissive manner, an attitude that continues until the novel's ending, and even precipitates it.

I've always linked two other poems in *Masks* with 'Are There Still Wolves in Pennsylvania?' These are 'On the Appalachian Trail' and 'Seventy Thousand Hillbillies'. Both have the poet's approval of people in a very particular area of the USA ironically commenting on how they are perceived in the rest of their country, and thus the world. Bush, on the face of it, appears adamant:

> But most places you go in Appalachia
> Heritage looks what
> it is all over:
> denizen tourism
>
> . . .
> once parochialism
>
> gets shown
> its own face
> in the mirror it's no
> use for anything
>
> This isn't hinterland Wales; these
> Pits aren't yet Labour museums
>
> 'On the Appalachian Trail:
> Eastern Kentucky' (1994a)

Bush locates his poems in particular yet still rather vague places – 'Arkansas' and 'Eastern Kentucky' – his 'Wales' is inexact. Perhaps he is reserving approval for populations who rejoice in the branding of 'hillbillies' and turn it on its head. And that 'parochialism' is implied for all of us:

> craftwork and local colourists
> look like the one sure
> future here too
>
> 'On the Appalachian Trail: Eastern Kentucky'

And:

> Maybe it's protective
> local colouring, hedged in by
> the Survivalists out in the bush

with their razor wire,
...
booby traps and bunkered arsenals

'Seventy Thousand Hillbillies' (1994a)

Both these poems lack the particularising art of Duncan Bush we find in 'Are There Still Wolves in Pennsylvania?'

In a letter to me, Ian Gregson writes: 'The sequence that concludes that volume [that is, *Masks*] . . . exposes the limits of American individualism, and how much that official ideology is compromised by an authoritarianism that can force its citizens to fight in a war that is entirely alien to them' (2023). The social comment, and political stance that might be implied by it in this work, is always present. Bush's politics is crucially and cleverly implicit in this ten-poem sequence set in America. The next chapter turns to Bush's strong European identity.

11

The Amsterdam Review (2004–6)

The *Amsterdam Review* is a literary magazine which Duncan Bush co-edited with P. C. (Paul) Evans. It appeared for three issues between 2004 and 2006, and is significant in what it shows about Duncan Bush as a writer. In writing this chapter, Paul Evans has been of great service, and with his permission I include two letters he has written to me. The first, from 2022, explains the origins of the *Amsterdam Review*, and offers his considered opinion of his experience with Bush:

> Re. Duncan and *The Amsterdam Review* . . . We spent a couple of days getting to know each other; Duncan had been one of the few Welsh poets from the Welsh old guard whose work I genuinely admired, but I'd never met him. We took him around the red light district in his dirty-old-man raincoat and Dai cap, and he spent the whole time commenting on the quality of the masonry of the buildings and the in-laid tiles of gargoyles, trading ships and cherubs.

(I note the complaint on social media, discussed in chapter 8, about Stew Boyle mentioning 'mansard roofs' when he should be conforming to 'working-class' stereotypes.) Paul Evans continues:

> on the day he was heading back to Luxembourg, we spent a couple of hours at the stylish/shabby Grand Cafe on the first platform of Amsterdam Central train station, waiting for Duncan's train; they have all of the clocks up on the wall there showing the different times in the major cities all over the world; a perfect place to be in transit. Duncan and I got to talking about

how we felt more rooted in a wider (high) European literature, than something narrowly British and English.

We talked about the various European poets and writers that we admired – Pavese, etc. and Duncan started telling me how well-connected he was (to Umberto Eco, etc.). So, we decided to pool our connections – my UK, Dutch, and European connections, Poetry International, and the international poetry festival (The Garden Party) that Sascha [Paul's partner] and I were organising at the Theatre Institute in Amsterdam, which gave us the money to have international poets translated, from which Duncan and I made selections for the magazine. Duncan was going to bring in most of the major European fiction and some poetry.

Here I imagine the two editors of the *Amsterdam Review* were trying to impress one another – an almost inevitable situation for such a new and ambitious publication. 'The first thing we did together was write the mission statement at the front of issue 1 and we kept to that as our guiding principle.' That statement runs:

The Amsterdam Review is a new magazine for European literature. It publishes high quality poetry, fiction, translations, essays and articles of literary interest by new and established authors.

The Amsterdam Review aims to encapsulate the cosmopolitan values of a European literary culture forged from a common classical tradition, continually renewed by avant-garde innovation, and founded in liberal and enlightened thought.

This occupies the fourth page. What the statement does not say is that all contributions should be, and were, in English or translated thus.

The first issue of the *Amsterdam Review* was published in 2004. The biographical note on Bush in this magazine is of interest. 'Duncan Bush is a poet and novelist. He has also published translations of Mallarmé, Baudelaire, Pavese and Pierre de La Prée.' Who? Bush's translations of this writer are published in the second issue of the *Amsterdam Review*. These are good poems. They certainly read like translations, or 'versions' by Duncan Bush. So good are they that the reader might wonder where Bush first encountered de La Prée's work. I had not heard of this writer before being introduced to him by his translator: de La Prée? A name associated with the French town of La Rochelle, amongst others. But then, neither had I encountered Victor Bal. Nor Isaac Babel. These are the central figures of *The Genre of Silence*. One is real, one fictional.

Also, I had not encountered 'Jay McGill', who, we are told by the *Amsterdam Review*, 'works in London and Paris'. Another prose work from the same source by McGill describes a photographic exhibition. Masquerading as essayist and poet 'Jay McGill', Duncan Bush contributes 'Avedon's Drifters', which subsequently appears under Bush's own name seven years later in *The Flying Trapeze* (2012), and is discussed in chapter 13.

P. C. Evans wrote to me (2022): 'Of course, Duncan must have overstated his connections a bit, we never got anything from Eco or Kundera, as he suggested, and most of his contributions – such as Pierre de La Prée – were written by himself, although he denied that at the time.' As to Paul Evans's final considerations of Duncan Bush's impersonations, he wrote a second letter to me (2023), in answer to my question:

> Q. Did you feel it mattered much when you discovered Duncan Bush was really 'Jay McGill' and 'Pierre de La Prée', considering that in Issue 2, McGill is both essayist and poet (thus he is credited with the essay 'Sebald's Itineraries' and the poem 'Avedon's Drifters'), while de La Prée has three poems, 'A Season in Sarajevo', 'Douce France' and 'Poem at Eleven O'Clock'?

Paul answered:

> Duncan sent me Jay McGill's 'Paragliding and the Art of Serious Fiction' for the first issue. It was a good essay that attacked the lack of risk-taking in UK publishing. I only found out that McGill didn't exist when I phoned Duncan to ask for his bio. The McGill persona probably allowed Duncan to be more openly critical of UK publishing than the novelist Duncan Bush could have been. McGill was a good writer, so we kept publishing him. I think if McGill were writing now, he would be very good on the culture wars in UK publishing.

> Pierre de La Prée was a different case. Duncan told me that Pierre was real ... I don't think it matters that Pierre doesn't exist. Duncan felt the need for this kind of poet in French literature, so he invented him. Our readers are probably still waiting for Pierre's first collection.

While Duncan Bush contributed to the *Amsterdam Review* in these personae, he also wrote under his own name. The first issue of the *Amsterdam Review* contains Duncan Bush's prose work 'Death Will Come and It Will Have Your Eyes', a reflection on Cesar Pavese, together with Bush's own translations of seven of Pavese's poems, his 'Last poems: 11th March to 10th April, 1950'. Bush's translations of Pavese have cropped up in various places, but there has been no dedicated collection, as was once mooted. Are the translations any good? My lack of Italian precludes a judgement. But as poems in English they certainly serve. The article by Nerys Williams, a Welsh-speaking poet and critic, 'Duncan Bush and the Parasitic Art' (2002), provides a careful reading of Bush's translations and versions.

In his prose reflection on Pavese, Bush creates an evocative picture of Turin: 'Raw, breathable mist rising from the Po. A more venomous one from the heavy traffic across its bridges' (2004a). And in his translation of Pavese, from 'The Cats Will Know':

> Still the rains will fall
> on your smooth pavements
>
> (2004a)

He visits the Hotel Roma where Pavese committed suicide (Bush is also aware that Primo Levi killed himself in Turin, as he states in the first issue):

> The man behind the counter had an interesting face – elegant in feature; yet as savage as a caricature in the glossy blackness of his hair, the thickness of his eyebrows, the blueness of the well-shaved jaw and the creamy pallor of the skin. It was the face of a small-part actor who's been in many films but whose name you've never known.

> When I mentioned Pavese a polite expression of well-rehearsed grief appeared on his face, as if to show it still pained the employees of the Hotel Roma to be reminded that such a man had come to such an end in their establishment. It was so patently a trained reflex that I wondered just how many literary pilgrims, programme makers, biographers or ghouls turn up here in the average year to ask the number of the room in which Pavese died – or even go as far as to book it; try out the bedsprings and contemplate that last view from the window. (2004a)

The essay contains the reasons Duncan Bush was fascinated by Pavese:

> He was at the height of his reputation and his powers. And it was the year that he committed suicide . . . Pavese is also one of those writers other writers learn from: about inwardness and indirection, ordinariness and subtlety. One thing is certain: there is nothing remotely like him in English, and few writers in any language can match that unique, disconsolate undertow of the sadness of all things which his best work reveals. (2004a)

(I compare the poems 'Living' and 'Evening', from *Salt*; Bush's own writing reveals this 'disconsolate undertow of the sadness of all things'.)

Bush follows the career of the actress Constance Dowling, loved, fatally, by the poet. That love, burning 'away, slowly, like green wood' (as Pavese puts it in a poem), 'tortured by the uncertainty of everything' (2004a). Typically, Bush views her through a film she appears in: *Up in Arms*, a Danny Kaye 'vehicle'. Also filmic is his description of the concierge of the Hotel Roma, quoted above: how carefully that man is portrayed. As ever, Bush is here using his avid appetite for film and screen to picture 'real' people. Like Bush's visit to Turin and the Hotel Roma, and his translations of Pavese, this all constitutes a homage paid by one writer to another.

This is from 'The Cats Will Know', dated 10 April, 1950, its title originally in English, and possibly the final verses of what Duncan Bush considered Pavese's last poem:

The cats will know,
face of springtime;
and the light rain,
the hyacinth-coloured dawn
that tears open the heart
of those with no more hope of you;

are the sad smile
which you smile alone.
There'll be other days;
other voices, other awakenings.
We'll suffer through the dawn;
face of springtime.

(2004a)

Duncan's last volume of his own poetry does not include any of these Pavese translations. (Possibly copies of the *Amsterdam Review*, issues 1–3 from 2004–5, remain obtainable from P. C. Evans.)

In his interview with Richard Poole, Bush states:

> I did most of my Pavese translations one summer, to keep my hand in, when I was too busy to be working on anything new of my own. I did them sitting in a shaded place in the garden in Gravesend, Kent, where we lived at the time, after a morning in London teaching Italian students English. But most of my translations have in common the recognition that being able to work my way through certain poems in the language in which they were written is not enough of an homage. (Poole, 1992a)

In issue 2 of the *Amsterdam Review*, Bush writes, again as Jay McGill, an appreciation of W. G. Sebald in 'Sebald's Itineraries'. Here, I feel, he might have been writing about himself. But I believe that all writing might be construed as autobiographical. Even, or especially, biography. 'Through Sebald's work we suffer again the affliction of never being anywhere at rest; longing always to be in another place; in sum, the existential sorrow of being whoever and wherever we are' (2005c). These words are written by Duncan Bush, who spent more than his first thirty years in 'rented rooms'. They are very similar,

I find, to Bush's thoughts on Pavese that appeared in the *Amsterdam Review*'s first issue: 'the terseness of Pavese's diary entries on the subject [of his relationship with Constance Dowling] is such as to perform the office of indiscretion to the prying, necrophile gaze of biographical posterity' (2004b). And it's himself as much as anyone he blames here, both Pavese and Sebald appearing eternally disconsolate. But that was why Duncan Bush was attracted to both writers.

The *Amsterdam Review* provided an outlet for Duncan's writing – both as himself, and as Jay McGill and Pierre de La Prée. But his involvement was also as joint editor. Paul Evans's letter to me (2022) commented on his strengths as an editor.

> The best thing about Duncan's editorship was his internationalist attitude and his refusal to compromise. Tony Ward of Arc wanted to take over as co-publisher; I think we credited Arc with the second or third issue. Arc would have given us greater reach, but Tony wanted to be co-editor and push his poets. Duncan was having none of it because the mag was all about quality and independence.

But the letter also notes problems, which Evans claims contributed to the short life of the magazine:

> The slightly negative side was that Duncan would foster old grudges through the mag . . . Also, we had the deal that both of us had to like a contribution, otherwise it wouldn't be accepted.
>
> By the end, I had total financing from the Dutch Foundation for Literature, but I was generating and commissioning almost all the content, apart from Duncan's self-written stuff; my Dutch publisher Wagner & Van Santen was producing the mag, but I was dealing with all the subscribers and people submitting work. I'd make a pre-selection and post it down to Luxembourg, and then Duncan and I would do the editing over the phone.
>
> Duncan loved being the editor of an international magazine, it was in all of his reading bio's at that time, and he organised the odd launch for himself, such as at the Hay on Wye festival. I arranged for some other poets to go over to back him up. But I was inundated with work for the mag, and Duncan really only wanted to be a selector of contributions, when we basically needed all hands on deck to grow the mag. We were getting

> contributors and subscribers from all over the world, the financing was in place, but I put it on the back burner after the third issue (meaning to pick it up later), but then the kids came.
>
> . . .
>
> The last time I saw Duncan was at a 'First Thursday' [event in Cardiff] when I was there with you, and Amy [Wack, Seren poetry editor] introduced him as the poet and editor of *The Amsterdam Review* [5 June 2012]. He was a bit frosty.

P. C. Evans might not be averse to hearing from other possible co-editors for the now defunct, yet possibly not extinct, *Amsterdam Review*. I would imagine, in an ideal world, co-editorship might be taken on by an ambitious academic or hopefully 'maverick' poet or novelist. (However, there now exists (2024) a different journal titled *Amsterdam Review*, founded in 2022 by Daniel Nemo.)

The third and final issue credits editors P. C. Evans and Duncan Bush, but notes the involvement of the publisher Arc. The submissions address remained Paul Evans's private home, but for some reason this issue does not contain the original mission statement (which actually occurs only in the first issue).

The *Amsterdam Review* provides a fascinating glimpse of the ambitions and scope of the middle-aged Duncan Bush's writing.

12

Now All the Rage (2007)

This, which proved to be Bush's third novel, arrived from a hitherto unknown press, Colophon. Actually, this is Duncan Bush himself, as the Godre Waun Oleu, Ynyswen address it bears makes clear. Considering its subject, that is eerily appropriate. 'Fame is an acid bath. Yet many seek immersion there. The wish to be famous is a modern religion, in that only personal fame might make sense of the world, celebrity's virtual DNA promising immortality' (Minhinnick, 2014).

Duncan Bush was as much interested in the processes by which fame is 'achieved' as he was by its lack; thus, his haiku-form long poem 'Hollywood Wildlife' (uncollected). This, from its section 'Vistas of Los Angeles: by Day':

Incognitii burn
For even an extra fifteenth-
Of-a-second's fame;

That windscreen wiper's
Arc of a glimpsedness in the sweep
Of motorcade crowds,

Faces brief as snow
Or tickertape – but on film!

(2007b)

This wish, this quest for 'fame', now a global delirium, fills the space that might be occupied by determination to serve, to contribute. To make art.

Step forward Guy Hughes, already an artist. But not a famous artist. Hughes suffers the frustration of the middle-aged painter who feels overlooked. Yet beneath the rage, and supporting it? A reef of boredom. Guy Hughes's boredom is different from the exasperated, then ominous, then psychotic frustrations of Stew Boyle, and also from the ennui Bush delighted in with his choice of translations from French. Hughes lives in what might be Cardiff or Newport suburbia, the novel opening with a car alarm disturbing the peace of pre-dawn in a quiet street.

Typically, for a 'true artist', Guy Hughes can sometimes forget whether he has eaten or not, so profound are his creative spasms. And Guy Hughes also enjoys pornography. He knows that porn, like everything else, is there to make money from him. Whilst keeping him quiet. But if he is clever he can also use it as fuel for his fantasies and his art. Pornography is responsible for the novel's pivotal moment. This occurs when Mrs Hughes discovers Mr Hughes in a luxurious act of self-pleasurement. Readers might view this as Portnoyish farce, but for Guy Hughes an interrupted fantasy is no laughing matter.

Because Guy Hughes is quite the fantasist. He was born, like Duncan Bush, in 1946, and knows time is passing. In his imagination, Guy is a brilliant polymath, arriving from nowhere to dominate the UK art scene. In his public appearances, such as *Desert Island Discs*, the tardiness of his celebrity is discussed. Perhaps there is hope for 62-year-old wannabes.

Many people will find Guy tedious, if not repellent. I find him a clever satire on modern masculinity, because men might admire him. Why? Hughes is driven by his own art, is moderately 'successful', and has a healthy hatred for that suburbia where he lives and the mores of the college that employs him. And maybe, above all, because he understands he is no world-beater. Yet moderate success seems no success at all. Celebrity is a class-A narcotic. Fantasy must be intensified to feed the addiction. Thus Hughes's belated first book, *Fragments From a Life*, has alerted Hollywood. And yes, it is Hughes who will direct. And star. A fawning Jeremy Paxman, chairing its Hay Festival launch, describes Hughes as a 'national treasure'. But just who is this paragon?

Hughes reveals his origins when he addresses the Hay hagiographers, but his hour in the grandest pavilion starts late. For this, Paxman blames their helicopter pilot, though the audience might suspect it was a crisp Bordeaux at Llangoed Hall (a notable restaurant for celebrity guests at the Hay Festival, such as former USA president Bill Clinton and Paul McCartney). Clearly, discussion of their shared projects has delayed these good friends. Peter Florence, first Hay Festival director, or his successors, must have been seething.

Duncan enjoyed the real Hay Festival, and Hay-on-Wye itself. This is taken from his Facebook site, 31 May, 2012 (and also reveals his love of cricket):

> It's Festival time again . . . I come to Hay at all times of the year, for the butcher's and the open market and the bookshops. But driving there today along the usual small roads with verges thick with cow parsley and hedgerows white with may, it's at its loveliest. Hay-on-Wye is May-on-Wye . . . I'm reading tomorrow night with Patrick McGuinness, and hugely looking forward to it. (He and I have corresponded often but never met.)
>
> Today Worcestershire asparagus at the open-air market, and a learned discussion with the stallholder and a customer, who grows it and has his own way of cooking it. Asparagus and Herefordshire strawberries are also part of the Hay experience – what the literary last week of May is in this glorious part of the world . . .
>
> Meanwhile, on the far side of Herefordshire, on this 31st of the month, Nick Compton [see Dennis Compton] is hoping for a last opportunity to bat at Worcester and get the 59 runs he needs to score a thousand runs in May. (Did even his grandfather do that? I dunno . . .)
>
> Isn't Summer wonderful?

It is not difficult to see through Hughes's fantasy. Yet Guy is plausible. The talk he gives at Hay mesmerises his audience, and maintains the reader's attention. Until that reader realises that Duncan Bush is dissecting us all with a satirical scalpel. And that Guy Hughes's oration is a monumental piss-take:

> All have been revealed, and all know it. Revealed not to others but privately, to themselves, and, among those who had come there as couples, to their partners. All their past lives; their furtive lusts or brash flirtations, every promiscuity of thought and act, and every suspicion of another's infidelity, have been exposed. (2007a)

Thus *Now All the Rage* is about delusion. Because of this, it is also sometimes very funny. Guy is able to turn his masturbation into art.

> Now it had the graphic quality he wanted. All art renders homage to its origins. Here the crudeness of his line . . . recalled the drawings on walls and doors in public toilet cubicles . . .
>
> Seen from above, the man going under the lintel of the doorframe was now naked, and preceded by his own erect phallus gripped in one hand. Pale-stemmed, violet-tipped, like a horizontal asparagus. (2007a)

Clearly, 'asparagus' was another favoured word. And in his 'Paris Haikus' (2005b), and, like all the other haikus in that edition of the magazine, awaiting appearance in a collection, Bush determinedly uses another one of his 'unusual' words. This, from 'Estampes Erotiques':

> The erotic prints
> Swell grossly ithyphallic
> To their blunt male point
>
> (2005b)

In terms of haiku, Bush seems to have counted his syllables. And it's a mark of his teasing good humour that he can use 'canicular' and 'umbilicises' in the five haikus that form 'At Giverny' (again 2005b).

Overall, in *Now All the Rage*, we find ourselves imprisoned within an imaginary world within another imaginary world, until some person from Porlock, usually by telephone, intrudes upon the trance. As Bush writes in 'Hollywood Wildlife':

> nobody's sure
> who's no-one in this town, or
> whether that might change
>
> (2007b)

We're in the world of screens, frames and images that always fascinated the writer. But apart from Hughes, there are no characters of real interest, although Terry Goss is credible. 'Goss has become "Dean of Fine Arts". He had . . . started his teaching life as a painter and a maker of experimental films . . . Gradually the youthful delusion of talent . . . had deserted him' (2007a). But Terry Goss is finally 'triumphant'. He marries Barbara, Guy's wife. And when the couple go to bed together it is 'an act of self-vindication and revenge'. Or, this might be another part of the overriding element of life in this novel.

Because the point of *Now All the Rage* is the importance of delusion. When Hughes is absent from the text we miss his self-obsessed propulsion, as Bush describes what has really occurred. (The same applies to *Glass Shot* on the rare occasions we are not inside Stew Boyle's head, listening to his manic soliloquy.) That's when the register changes to post-coital clarity. Thus, with this in mind, *Now All the Rage* ends neatly.

But knowing that Duncan died in 2017 because of bowel cancer, I pause at the 'misfortune . . . defecatory in nature', familiar to many of us, in 'The Quick and the Very Quick and the Dead' chapter. Bush knew that everything could, and should, be written about. *Now All the Rage* was his final novel; the next chapter discusses his last poetry collection, *The Flying Trapeze*.

13

The Flying Trapeze (2012)

Duncan Bush's last volume of poetry before his death was the first such collection since *Midway* (1997), a significant interval in a writer's life. However, I remember Bush telling me at its launch, in Cardiff's Chapter Arts Centre, on 5 June, 2012, that the volume could have been significantly larger, and he expected another volume from the same publisher in the not too distant future. At the time of writing (2024), that volume is yet to materialise. But Bush's dedication, written in the flyleaf of *The Flying Trapeze*, 'To Robert who published so many of these poems, Chapter, 5.vi.2012', is accurate. I accepted them while I was editor of the magazine *Poetry Wales*.

Clearly, Bush's confidence in his own linguistic capability had grown, as this volume includes three poems with versions in both English and French. (Before publication he ensured his French was expertly checked.)

Duncan Bush's poems in the period since *Midway* had been published for the most part individually, thus it was only the appearance of this book that proved what Duncan Bush's late poetic concerns had been. European travel has now become global, with several poems about Australia. Yet we are already familiar with his writings on America, also present. Europe is viewed from 'The Rom out of Romania', 'East Side Story' (in Berlin), 'Douce France' and 'A Season in Sarajevo'. Some characteristics of Bush's writing remain throughout his career – the use of lists, attention to detail, and enthusiasm for interesting words. But some later poems show new developments – a greater concision, the use of the haiku form.

Despite Bush's intention to deliver a collection of translations of Cesar Pavese, I was surprised none of these appear in *The Flying Trapeze*. However, there exist earlier Bush translations of Pavese: 'Agony' and 'Those Who Were There', from 1982, in *Poetry Wales*; and 'Agony', 'Fatherhood' and 'Revolt', collected in *Aquarium*. But I find it disappointing that *The Flying Trapeze* does not include his impressions of Turin and translations from the Italian of Pavese brought together over seventeen pages in the first issue of the *Amsterdam Review* (2004), under the overall title 'Death Will Come and It Will Have Your Eyes' (see chapter 11). There was an obvious precedent for this in *Midway*, which contains the seventeen-page prose autobiographical essay, 'Lash LaRue and the River of Adventure'. As Bush was a writer who had always believed in fluidity of genre, such a decision would not have been surprising. I propound that Bush acted thus because he was anticipating his writings on Pavese sharing a single collection.

But instead of this work we have eight pages of the interminable 'Still Living at Sixteen', which I published in *Poetry Wales*. I supposed it an experiment but am disappointed to read it again in *The Flying Trapeze* at the expense of more well-achieved work. A great deal of this poem reads like a catalogue:

> Luxembourg is a small country
> famous for three things: cheap booze. Cheap
> cigs, cheap petrol
>
> (2012b)

Nevertheless, I was particularly pleased to use 'Couch Grass', which subsequently has been published in the anthology *100 Poems to Save the Earth* (Brigley and Evans, 2021). This displays the poet's love of gardening and plants, and I have always admired its conclusion, for how Bush's eye extends sight from his own garden into a view of the whole world:

> Gloved, you straighten
> shaking soil;

Perseus brandishing

the Medusa head

Which leads to a powerful conclusion:

underground
it's already rife

as new rumour in deltas
of knotted fibres;
coarse white jointed net

that will spread
choking
the earth

if not The Earth
aswing
in its old swing bag of meridians

(2012b)

A reader of *Midway* will be prepared for the poet attempting to rid his garden of the plant; see 'And Suddenly it's Evening', in which a 'smoking couch-grass fire' burns:

slow
grey and yellow-sulphurous.

(1997a)

The title poem of *The Flying Trapeze* is a comment on both fame and nationalism, Bush quoting William Saroyan (1934) calculating the numbers of Assyrians left in the world, via an Assyrian barber in California. Also present here is 'Douce France'; a French-language version by Bush himself is twinned with it. This too is a comment on nationalism, with the poet in explicit parts of France describing the colour blue, then expanding his view historically:

Finest of all colours
which please me is the blue
with a violet tint in it

only ever glimpsed
going past
down some 'D' road in the Var

or the Meurthe-et-Moselle
. . .
and something
surges back

to thoughts of all
the boys from these villages
. . .
gone for soldiers

(2012b)

This is a poet showing delicacy and at his painterly best, who found, late in his writing career, liberation in the haiku or seventeen-syllable verse form. And for expert concision, which such writing demands, read 'Obituary Page'. This is the whole poem:

The classic photo:
Brown eyes; lids hooded; saurine:
The banded trilby

At an ad-man's tilt:
Saul Bellow died yesterday.
The rest move up one.

(2012b)

No greater tribute from Bush is possible. For those whom Duncan Bush admired, go to those he translated or those whose lives he celebrated. Thus, this is the whole of 'Rimbaud's Childhood':

I.
Season of Sadness;
Heart like a town the circus
Never visited.

2.
Eternal Sundays
Of these drab provincial towns;
Even the blues wan.

(2012b)

From *The Flying Trapeze* it's impossible not to re-read 'In Memory of Basil Bunting' with its furious blast at those who seek prominence and 'career' reward:

'Ignore the critics', Basil Bunting advised,
the day I interviewed him. 'And never respond
to reviews, especially good ones'. He was spry
in his old-gold waistcoat and professorial beard.
He wrote Briggflatts and lyrics of a delicate
beauty, but much in draft was balled for bin or grate. And so he died,
in his parents' Quaker faith in
the dignity of held silence amid the drab
paucities of old age on a state pension, and a sense
that the careers of glib paravails – hyperactive
mediocrities and untiring networkers,
website hitmen and other stars of lowest
magnitude who know that poetry is just one
more branch of publicity – bloom in a rummage
of printed matter fit only for grasping in
an outside lavatory built over a lime-pit.

(2012b)

Here, Bunting is idealised by Bush as to how a writer should behave and live. It is this anger that becomes the satire of the novel *Now All the Rage*, and was a prominent theme in the writer's later work.

'Donald George Bradman, 1907–2001' is familiar Bush territory – the scrupulous attention to detail, the naming of places:

> Still young, a boy vignetted
>
> in an old tinted cigarette-card photo enlarged
> from a team grouping; he wore a dove-grey
>
> club blazer with rose grosgrain edging
> collar and lapels, the misty corrugated-iron stand
>
> at Bowral or Goulburn behind him
> . . .
> All the records unknown; and intact.
>
> (2012b)

That 'unknown' is telling. Donald Bradman flourished prior to our modern screen culture, its constant replays from every angle we have learned to crave. Duncan Bush, moreover, was a cricket-lover, and I remember his pride in recounting to me the leg-spin exploits of one of his sons, leg-spinners being the 'eccentrics' of cricket, supposedly possessing ability to conjure 'unorthodox' and mysterious deliveries, such as the 'googly', 'chinaman' or 'doosra'. In 'Living in Real Times', in *Masks*, I'm sure Bush pauses because it's leg-spinner Shane Warne who is 'looping wristspin in at some tailender' (1994a). Even for those who understand only the rudiments of cricket, such a sight was, at least for some of those, unmissable.

'East Side Story', about the 'new Europe' after the Berlin Wall came down, reveals Bush at his politically keenest, especially here with its stun grenades:

> The latest babushka doll's a Yeltsin drunk –
> Creased eyes, silver quiff, all phoney 'yo-ho-ho'
> Inside him is Gorbachev – that balding, birth-
> marked pate;
> then – face like a frost-corrupted swede –

Brezhnev, and next size down, 'dinky' Uncle Joe . . .
Last, inmost and tiniest of this bear's litter

of hardliners or tools, the bearded Lenin, shrunk
from the gigantism of his civic statuary
to the runt. (All five for 'Zwanzig Mark, bitte!')

(2012b)

Bush's short poems improved as he grew older and learned how to sculpt his words – to trust the precision of his eye. This last collection has several notable examples. This from 'Wear':

Even in Rome you note
Not St Peter's mild gaze but
The patina of

Kisses yellowed on
His hallux, the bright strap to
That brazen sandal.

(2012b)

Concern for concision became more important towards the end of his life, as might be construed from the 'unpublished and uncollected' work described in the next chapter.

But also notable here, in this last published collection, is 'Avedon's Drifters', in which Bush seeks out a photographic exhibition in New York showing the photographs of Richard Avedon (1924–2004). This originally appeared in the second issue of the *Amsterdam Review*, as written by 'Jay McGill'. I feel this an emblematic poem of Duncan Bush, powerfully revealing his humanitarian sympathies. For me it's noteworthy that the version in this collection is unchanged from the original in the *Amsterdam Review*, as Bush was a constant redrafter.

After wall on wall of
The important, fashionable or glamorous

famed pictures of the famous
. . .
      in the last gallery space
that we confront
Richard Avedon's portraits
of sky-eyed losers –

these shrunken bellied rueful old boys
dapper in Western-style duds

(2012b)

These drifters and 'itinerants' are encountered in 'Hobbs, New Mexico, Chloride, Nevada, Golden, Colorado, with a gleam of wildness not wholly dulled'. The poet wishes to celebrate 'these vagabond drinkers or feckless workhands', and gives both their names and the places in which they were encountered by the photographer (2012b). 'Avedon's Drifters' is clearly the work of the same poet who wrote 'Navvies' and 'Quarries at Dinorwic' in *Salt*. It also is another example of Bush's love of naming and listing, not merely for the powerful impact of repetition, but for its commemorative value, as with 'In the Aftermath', from the pamphlet *Black Faces, Red Mouths*. Duncan Bush is rightly sure that this is an effectively dramatic and poetic combination. These things, Bush insists, must be known. Thus, 'In the Aftermath':

Cottonwood
Polmaise
Aberpergwm
Ashington
Treforgan.

(1985a)

This technique is also used in 'At the News of Proposed Pit Closures', which is one of two poems 'dropped altogether', because thought 'unsalvageable', from the reprinting of *Aquarium*, as quoted in *The Hook*:

> Always just the names
> that make the paper:
> Coegnant. Aberpergwm. Brynlliw-Morlais.
> Ty Mawr Lewis. Even
> Britannia

(1997c)

Such technique, also revealed by this final collection, links Bush's early with later poems, especially 'Avedon's Drifters':

> Lives gone awry in America, though each
> in Whitman's words
> was a child once
> sleeping in his mother's bedroom
>
> And we are moved
> by these faces, by their grievous
> dignity; we are halted
> in passing (see how scrutinising faces
>
> among a queue-dense wet-Sunday public are
> ennobled by sympathy:
> by a troubled intentness
> this on the faces of urbanite Noo Yawkers
>
> who in the pavement's flow ignore daily
> and all week the sight
> of other persons
> adrift, deracinate or feral).
>
> Yet something too shrinks back
> at these photographs;
> some diffidence or
> delicacy;
>
> since which of us could imagine singling out
> each out-of-luck stranger

in a bar forecourt or a roadside;
brokering the fee for the shots?

Perhaps in all human empathy,
all art; a ruthless prurience lies visible
like a watermark
at a certain angle to the light.
. . .
and bigger than life-size
are these vagabond drinkers
or feckless workhands
whom ordinarily the tactful eye slides past

(2012b)

Duncan Bush, here himself camera-like, as observant of Avedon's portraits as of the New York public. The poet identifies 'grievous dignity' in the photographer's subjects, but then he looks and thinks more closely and identifies a 'ruthless prurience' in Avedon himself. And thus in himself, for composing a poem about the whole experience.

The poem concludes with Bush again observing both the portraits and the people who have paid to view the exhibition:

undependable or disappointment-wounded
sons or husbands
of the fugitive kind; caught
before they edge away out of focus again:

guys of whom all their lives it was said
that they were never, ever there.

(2012b)

The Flying Trapeze concludes with a poem readers might find puzzling. Why 'Back in Arcadia'? I cannot recall ever having been there with Duncan Bush, who has a tremendous lyric gift, but whose natural environments are usually apple orchards or gardens in Gravesend, France or Luxembourg, such as described in 'Shrikes at Jaulny' (*Midway*):

> 38 in the balcony's shade,
> the orchids over but our hayfield
> still uncut, and teeming
>
> (1997a)

While, with 'Back in Arcadia', we await familiar seasonal orderliness:

> Back in Arcadia the trees
> Are always in full leaf

I note the upper case for first words of lines here. Bush liked to vary his approach, as he was never predictable. Yet the collection's final poem ends resolutely:

> Between the echo and its answer
> Pastoral is born, the ravaged fruit
> Drops, the season's over.
>
> (2012b)

Just like that. Meanwhile, Bush's essay 'On Matthew Arnold and Pastoral' notes: '*Yet the blackest, most Blakean mill-town arose among fields or in reach of woods . . . and until fairly recently, London, most dystopian and sprawling of metropolises, could be walked out of on a morning*' (2002c). But considering time and population growth, readers today might suggest that other global cities appear far more 'sprawling' and 'dystopian'.

Knowing the poet, I search for irony in 'Back in Arcadia' and would be happy to be directed towards it. So I turn to 'Cider Orchard Story, near Pershore: Verbatim' and decide maybe I should keep seeking. The sculpted environment Bush seemed to yearn for is clearly present in 'Abandoned Orchard', almost a companion piece to 'Cider Orchard Story':

and planted his trees well-spaced
in grass mown back to tousled lawn to sit out on
on summer weekends.

(2012b)

I think, perused again, Bush would have excised the second 'on'.

The Flying Trapeze contains well-achieved individual poems, yet is not as ambitious or successful as either *Masks* or *Midway*. The pages it allots to 'Still Living at Sixteen' would have been better filled by some of his Pavese translations. I believe a further volume, of both uncollected and 'new' poems, would be a significant publication and would complete a powerful poetic oeuvre, as yet incomplete. These poems are discussed in the next chapter.

14

Unpublished and uncollected poems

In January 2021, Annette Weaver provided me with a collection of her husband Duncan Bush's unpublished poems and prose.[1] Inevitably this includes what seem to be earlier versions of some published poems; poems that he did not consider publishable; and poems that, had he lived, would probably have been published. In fact, three of these poems have now been published in *Poetry Wales* (Bush, 2023).

This chapter discusses these unpublished poems, together with those that were published but have not been included in any of the collections discussed in previous chapters. Again, these are a mixed bunch, including poems that Duncan had indicated might appear in collections (in particular his Pavese translations and essay); poems that he had decided to not include in collections; and just one poem published after his last collection.

The three poems first published in *Poetry Wales* are 'Robert Lowell', 'My Father's Tools' and 'La France Éternelle'. In 'Robert Lowell', Bush makes much of his own scrupulous reading of poetry in general:

> If
> Milton brought a loud-hailer
> into poetry
>
> – now clear, now strident,
> Joshua's brash, brass trumpet
> in its bell – Lowell's

urged an insistence
of brazen confessional,
unforgiven, unshriven –

words hissed or declaimed,
half-fraught, half-boastful. His eyes
saw what his hand did,

then it thumped his chest
and said so. We also serve
who just sit and wait.

(2023)

Robert Lowell is another of Bush's American literary heroes (Saul Bellow and Elmore Leonard were others). And I compare this 'new' but published work with 'West 86th Street', from *The Flying Trapeze*, both poems replete with details of brand-named clothes. I note Lowell's 'Turnbull and Asser shirt'. Bush admired style, whether in Robert Lowell himself or 'elderly / well-off Jewish men who live on New York's Upper West Side' (2012b). (For further evidence of the poet's love of stylistic appearance, and what it signifies, see below in the 'Paris Haikus'.)

There are two versions of 'Robert Lowell'. It seems the author thought twice about his description of Lowell's final years at the poem's conclusion, and cut it from the second draft.

One of Duncan Bush's strengths is his delighted adumbration of the brands, the names, the words they comprise. (A favourite is 'haft'.) He is forever consciously salvaging such terms by using them in poetry. This is discoverable throughout his later poems, nowhere more distinctively than in 'My Father's Tools'.

His Rabone-Chesterman
66 foot builder's
tape stands propped
on a shelf of my books.

(2023)

Part of Bush's urgency here is his own autobiography, as suggested by his father's life. Possibly 'My Father's Tools' was written after Bush's diagnosis for cancer.

To Duncan Bush, such detail must always be significant. The father's decisions become the poet's. That builder's tape adorned a shelf filled with the poet's own books. What craft went into its making? I can hear the reader asking. And where is that builder's tape now, I wonder? (Annette Weaver informs me she possesses it.)

'My Father's Tools' has prompted a discussion on Facebook about 'working-class poetry', especially from writers such as Cardiff's Topher Mills, recalling his own father's roofing work and the use of measuring tapes in awkward locations.

'La France Éternelle', the third of the recently published poems by Duncan Bush, is familiar territory, similar to other poems, especially 'Douce France' in *The Flying Trapeze*. Again, the imagery of 'blue with a violet tint in it', 'that matchless blue surrounding big white capitals', as in a faded Dubonnet sign (2023). And once more, the poet's eye for detail ignites the poem.

Duncan Bush is also fascinated by ennui. Or, more truthfully, boredom. This is how *Glass Shot* begins, with Stew Boyle's exasperated listlessness, a man apart from his wife and children on an Easter bank holiday, watching too familiar telly. This ennui is really the subject of 'La France Éternelle', and often notable in his working-class Cardiffians. Collected in *The Hook* are longish poems, such as 'The Quarries at Dinorwic' and 'Navvies', which predate work like the unpublished 'Bronze Age' and 'My Father's Tools', but also explicitly ponder workers' identities. These are an unignorable link between the books and the unseen pieces.

This connection between old work and new requires acknowledgement. These concerns were eternal for Duncan Bush. There is often optimism and scrupulous attention to detail in these later poems, despite a few which are bleaker. 'Under the Beacons', in the unpublished poems, is a grim physical description of Wales, probably viewed from Bush's home in Ynyswen. It appears to have become 'Primal Landscapes', which appeared in the *TLS* not long before

Bush's death. Here are familiar concerns but displayed in an especially jaundiced manner:

New South Wales still boasts
The Outback. But what's old south
Wales got?
'Out the back'.

Views of bare hills, grey
rain up the valley like net
curtains blowing at

an open window,
drab-decrepit housing-stock
built at the edge of

impoverished scrubland,
rush-tussocked grazing (Grade 5
Agricultural):

those starveling skewbalds
– some local cowboy's posse
loosed with blue-stained ewes

And:

Pumps stilled, pits flooded,
N.U.M. lodges dispersed
to Walmart-style jobs:
poverty's a stain
like a birthmark, or rain-mould
down a bedroom wall.

(2017)

'Primal Landscapes' is built around a bilious vocabulary: potched, stagnancy, unkempt, squalor, famished, misanthropic, slatternliness, vermin-like, coprophile . . . Taken on its own this might indicate a loathing for a particular part of Wales. But I think I understand what motivates the writer here, and can also state the poem begins with an awful cliché ('Out the back' referencing Welsh outside toilets) and, despite the careful versification, gets no better. It is as if Bush feels obliged to continue as he started. It is not dissimilar to 'Back to Cardiff':

The ponies are bowed
all day to crop subsistence; broken
by boredom; lashed
by slant grey rain.

(1986c)

'Primal Landscapes' is a poem bereft of the belief and energies displayed by the striking miners, now 'dispersed to Walmart-style jobs'. The implication is that it is this community spirit that once exemplified the best of 'old south Wales'.

Yes, I compare the poem, with its 'starveling skewbalds' to 'Back to Cardiff', but also to another 'horses' poem, Meic Stephens's 'Ponies, Twynyrodyn', in which the writer anticipates a change approaching for the better. A revolutionary sentiment, surely not only linguistic, but social. At least, to those who knew Stephens himself. Crucial is the time of life of both writers at composition.

Meic Stephens depicts the ponies 'shod with ice . . . manes stiff with frost and dung'. Merthyr Tydfil, Twynyrodyn and 'the valleys' gave them free rein, and still do:

they were the first tenants of these valleys;
their right to be here is freehold.

And the poem ends with an unashamed political and social statement:

These beasts are our companions,
dark presences from the peasant past;
these grim valleys our common hendre;
exiles all, until the coming thaw.

(1973)

Meic Stephens titled his first collection of poems *Exiles All* (1973), and Duncan Bush, in 'North-East of Eden', his column for *Poetry Wales*, writes: 'Exile . . . is a powerful force for the imagination' (2002b). Stephens titled his volume thus because he felt so many Welsh people are exiled from the Welsh language and an undefined 'Welsh way of life'. I believe Bush considered himself as often living 'in exile'. He deliberately chose to review the writings of 'exiles', such as Elias Canetti, and was fascinated at how 'exile' influenced, even directed, their lives. Whitchurch and north Llandaff in Cardiff, Gravesend in England, and places in France and Luxembourg didn't feel 'permanent' to the writer, despite his delineations of his home and gardens, such as appear in 'Shrikes at Jaulny' (*Midway*).

It is likely that Meic Stephens considered himself exiled from 'a Welsh way of life'; Duncan Bush seems implicitly exiled from 'the life of the writer'. If both conditions are indefinable, Stephens took the massive practical step of making Cymraeg the first language of his home and family. Bush, writing in his last book in both English and French, makes a less emphatic yet similar statement. He admired both Pavese and W. G. Sebald for what he termed their 'disgruntlement' or dissatisfaction. For me Duncan Bush was not 'rootless', but forever in a state of deliberate self-exile.

Among the poems that still remain unpublished, 'Edwardian' is worth an intent look, allowing Bush to contrast a photograph of 'Hardy and Elgar . . . who (seem to) / share one haircut and moustache / and identical three-piece suits / of hirsute, probably ginger, tweed' with 'every pimp and paravail on tv / who bare "gumshield grins"'. I look forward to its first publication.

The unpublished 'Myths of the Fall' centres, typically, on a particular watch, 'a Breguet hunter' 'sewn into a seam / in her grandfather's jacket'. The naming of the watch is vital to Bush and the poem, even though it appears:

> just a trinket
> from another life . . . from a distant land
> history had buried,
> even its graveyards ploughed in.

From its style this appears a late work, once more dealing with refugees, or at least the displaced, as do 'East Side Story' and 'The Rom out of Romania' (from *The Flying Trapeze*). This, again, from 'Myths of the Fall':

> a world which
> no longer exists and isn't shown on any
> map? Even the language
> they spoke then is now
> forgotten

Yes, Duncan Bush of the long historical gaze, as seen in another very late unpublished poem, 'Neolithic', in which this poet-connoisseur of physical labour and the nomenclature of tools, marvels at the people who 'cleared and broke the ground', built Avebury, though 'lacking the wheel or hoist':

> With flint axes
> & antler picks they
> cleared & broke the ground,
> with shoulder-blade shovels
> piled the mound

(I compare the poet's description of his father's work, as quoted in chapter 2, here.)

Bush notes that 'archaeology is mute' in providing the answers as to how this was achieved, evidence of the brutal anonymity of the world's workers in their 'infinity of labour'. Another response to the same issue is John Ormond's 'Cathedral Builders', who:

> Saw naves sprout arches, clerestories soar,
> Cursed the loud fancy glaziers for their luck;
> Somehow escaped the plague, got rheumatism,
> Decided it was time to give it up
>
> (1991)

One of the reasons Bush wrote was to provide actual names and identities for such people. His writings abound in determination to identify the forgotten, the erased, the ignored. For this writer, to name is to restore. Yes, Bush is his own archaeologist. The Cardiff mechanic, the Australian athlete, the victim of Stalin's pogroms, even that watch sewn into a seam, that measuring tape, that polished haft, are crucial details for this writer. For Duncan Bush, 'naming' is surely what literature means. His writing strives to identify the unnamed, and the implements those lost and unrecorded once might have used, as in poems such as 'Cold-Chisel':

> blunt,
> or delicate, by need,
>   you
> form and dismantle
> like good writing
> should;
>
> (1986c)

– or even in prose: 'that big kitchen knife', from *Glass Shot* (1991). As ever, the telling, but in this case, highly sinister, particularity.

Bush's unpublished 'The Calais Caricatures' suggests a link with the work of Harri Webb, the Welsh republican poet. In it he is severe, in a 'Gwlad, Gwlad' manner, but about the English this time. It is the poet's own words in the note below the poem:

> The people you see
> On the cross-channel ferry
> Leave you baffled to know
> How we ever beat Jerry:
>
> Corpulent grotesques
> On a day-ticket cruise
> To Calais's piled hangars
> Of bargain-price booze,

Faces out of Rowlandson
Or Cruikshank, timeless phizzes
From the gene-pool – though Jack
Sprat's now as fat as his missus

And both kids obese; meanwhile
On deck the smokers hunch
In a pariah huddle
For their nicotine lunch.

(The 'culture of dependency'
Is oral, not some social fiction –
Does weaning too late from
The dummy foster addiction?)

The straits are milky-calm
As for the Dunkirk rescues,
And the duty-free on board
Is cheaper than at Tesco's;

But we're missing something
We can't finger or name.
We feel that we're victims
But don't know who to blame.
We get by on brass neck
And we're steeled against shame,

Yet we're wistful for well-being
Like a squandered youth:
Gross-paunched and bloated in our skin,
We're squalid, ugly and uncouth.

The note attached reads:

What editor would be brave enough to take it?

Whereas a drawing representing people like those described would be widely acceptable under the usual allowances extended to visual representations of the grotesque (as in the newspaper cartoon), would a written version outrage the sensibility of all those who are sensitive on behalf of others, especially 'the vulnerable in society'?

Both note and poem must be considered tongue-in-cheek. Bush here might not be as successfully outrageous as Webb, but such previously unseen work makes it possible to compare these two poets' similarities. But why should it be strange? Both were 'Francophiles'. Both translated poetry from the French. Both published English and French versions of the same poems together. And both became impatient and then exasperated with the Welsh and the English.

This is Harri Webb's 'Please Keep Your Gog on a Lead':

> The mountain of Snowdon is barren and bleak,
> There are Gogs at the bottom and fogs at the peak,
> But it's worth the steep climb over boulders and bogs,
> For at least when you're up there you can't see the Gogs.
>
> (1995)

From Webb's *Collected Poems*, which contains a plethora of such barbs and squibs. Though maybe not as brutal as his infamous 'Anglomaniac Anthem':

> Oh, we're looking up England's arsehole;
> It's the prettiest view we know,
> It's the height of our ambition,
> It's where we want to go

There were twenty-six years age difference between Harri Webb and Duncan Bush.

I also believe Bush later in life was capable of versions, such as 'Wales 1970', which Webb adapts from the Breton of Paol Keineg, born 1944:

> Blinding unutterable unrestrained clamant
> entire starry close transparent
> snowy fugitive innumerable distant

incessant unhoped-for despised jubilant
feverish captive torn radiant.
A land heavily pregnant.

(1995)

Harri Webb experimented in translation, attempting versions of Sardinian, Breton, Catalan, French and Spanish (especially of Lorca), as well as Welsh-language poems. All of these are a dig in the ribs of monoglots who require reminding of 'minority' causes.

For me, Bush's later haikus resemble such writing as Webb's Keineg version. Not so much in Webb's political sentiment (although in this Breton version it is mild), but in the individual words, accumulating arbitrarily yet precisely as, yes, snow. And what word better sums up Bush's poetry, indeed, his whole attitude to writing, to words themselves, than 'clamant'? Bush was 'clamant' even before he began writing, revelling in his own vocabulary. Boastful? No. But energised.

Here is Bush from 'Paris Haikus': 'Images du Monde Flottant':

The floating world's sparse,
Full. The art's in leaving out.
White ground, black brushstroke
. . .
Their eyes are depthless;
The charged brush waits; eyelash fine.
The tidal wave's poised.

(2005b)

Webb also wrote 'The Conference', with which Bush might have agreed, if he had recalled Welsh Union of Writers open-mics.

They called themselves poets.
Ah well;
Bedbugs and butterflies
Are both insects.

(1995)

I am reminded here of published work in *The Genre of Silence*. Bush's explicit condemnation is voiced in 'Writers' Union Building, Moscow, 1937', but 'The Age of Rust' goes some way to provide balance:

> Our adult voices broke
> To a wheedle on the times'
> Skulduggery and paranoia.

With the more careful, even long-term hopeful:

> Now
>
> we know only those words
> persist which are self-seeding,
>
> perennial, unkillable as thistle
> or the slow green fire
>
> of couch-grass
>
> (1991)

Also as yet uncollected, 'At St Mary Redcliffe' appeared in *Poetry Wales*. Maybe Bush looked again at his amusing rhymes and thought better of it:

> My father sometimes voiced the claim
> That previous generations of our name

and

> Before the first Bush crossed the Severn,
> My ghostly forefathers in Bristol, Somerset or Devon
> Had eyes hard on the earth not heaven.
>
> (2003b)

The 'Paris Haikus', like 'Hollywood Wildlife' (see chapter 12), remain uncollected. For example: 'Solitary Aphrodisiac':

His single's table;
Cold Chablis poured, napkin chinned.
Two dozen oysters.

(2005b)

And 'The Artist's Waste-Bin':

His pencil-sharpener
Emptied: flutter of dead moths.
Scent of cedar-wood.

(2005b)

And 'Aux Jardins du Luxembourg':

Springtimes he'll miss; and
Apple-blossom, and the taste
of her kiss. And the
. . .
Hoverfly, drawn by
the whiteness of the paper
Where he's sketching this.

(2005b)

And 'The Game: Boulevard St Michel':

Girls on the Boul' Mich'
Beat. Drug-bruised eyes. Wash-tight jeans.
Thin loins of greyhounds.

(2005b)

'Vistas of Los Angeles: Night', from 'Hollywood Wildlife', has equally urban yet more expansive, indeed cosmic, use of the verse form:

Starry grid of lights
Best observed from Griffith Park
Observatory's fence

Or Mulholland Drive's
Mythic pull-in where teens park
To wet-pet or fuck;

Yet visible – vast
Circuit-board, the street-mapped glow –
From the moon's dry seas.

(2007b)

The 'Hollywood Wildlife' haikus share images, such as interviews with hopeful actors, a film lot, the Observatory and 'pull-in', with the film *La La Land*, directed by Damien Chazelle, but they predate the film, released in 2016. However, the film *Mulholland Drive* (2001) by David Lynch, might be a source. And I compare Nigel Jenkins's series of 'Cosmic Gnomes' (1998), with its fascinations with 'light' and astronomical imagery.

I believe that 'The Mexican Border at Night' was written about the same time as the 'Hollywood Wildlife' haikus. Roughly seventeen syllables per verse, this poem is stark:

Armed posts. The sense of
A compound. Then dark hills, folds
Aglitter with lights.

Like blankets smouldering.
Tijuana's pent-up slums;
The tourist highway

South skirts shanties, stench
Of sewage; drops to the coast's
Raw cement resorts.

(2010)

Brief images, individual words: almost skeletal construction is not unusual in Bush's poetry, but a way his verse might have developed.

Issue 2 of the *Amsterdam Review* contains three poems supposedly translated from the French of 'Pierre de La Prée', in reality Bush's own work. These are 'Douce France', 'A Season in Sarajevo' and 'Poem at Eleven O'Clock'. The first two appear in *The Flying Trapeze*, but the third is uncollected.

I will quote 'Poem at Eleven O'Clock' in its entirety here, as it represents aspects of Bush's poetry mentioned elsewhere in this volume, that is, selection of 'unusual' words, brand names, global reference and technical detail:

> And now the daily,
> the matutinal, the apothecary moment of
> the coffee
>
> intent ritual among
> its apparatus of chrome tubes, knobs, lights, levels
> tanks and taps
>
> the hermetic tins of
> roasted beans ground in Trieste
> and cane from Martinique:
>
> a veritable espresso extruded
> through a Krups machine vibrant at 15 bars of pressure
>
> leaving a sludge of leached mud in its scoop
> distilling to
>
> a tidemark
> of yellow foam
>
> and a swirl of the finest sand
> as a day at the beach does in the shower.
>
> Drink it. In a tiny cup.
> Then make another.
>
> (2005e)

Only available in the first issue of the *Amsterdam Review* are the ten pages of Bush's translations of Cesare Pavese's 'Death Will Come and It Will Have Your Eyes'. This is the penultimate poem that Pavese wrote, dated 4 April, 1950: 'The Night You Slept' is its original title, and Bush maintains the English wherever the author uses it:

The night resembles you too,
The distant night that weeps
Silently in the dark heart,
As weary stars wheel past.
Cheek touches cheek,
A cold shudder, someone
Struggles in alone, imploring you;
Lost within you; in your fever.

The night suffers and the dawn yearns,
Poor leaping heart.
O face now closed, dark grief,
Fever that saddens the stars;
Someone waits for dawn as you do;
Examining your face in silence.
You lie beneath the night
Like a horizon closed off and dead.
Poor leaping heart,
One distant day you'll be the dawn.

(2004a)

All of these poems concern Pavese's love for Constance Dowling. In Bush's 'Note' that concludes his essay and translations, he writes of internet references to Dowling, who 'starts her love affair – qualified in the website pages with the standard adjective "torrid" – with Pavese. Following his death, she returns to the United States in 1951' (2004a).

Probably Duncan Bush's last written poem is 'Barn Owl'. Because opportunity allowed, Annette Weaver read this several times at an event on 24 November, 2023, in Porthcawl, from handwritten drafts and preliminary typescripts:

Moon-bright mackerel cloud
The pearly undersides and
Down auxiliaries

Of an angel's wing
Arched vast over the dark land –
Genus rare to sight

As Tytonidae,
Snub-winged, heart-faced raptor with
Moth-furred claws and bill

Needing no moon but
Silence, whose glide and sudden
Drop, a shuttlecock's,

Pin the hectic heart
Of its fidgeting, scuttling
Prey then clutch it still.

Hunches on its post,
Then flies the tailed corpse to its
Brood, a ferrying ghost.

Once again, the seventeen-syllable stanza, and 'unusual' bird, while Bush particularises the type of owl with a satisfyingly rare word. And the author recalls his own 'For the Hawk Fallen', with its 'shuttlecock of pinions' (1994a).

The above poems and translations, with others, require collection and publication. For example, the five Bush versions of Pavese which I published in *Poetry Wales* (2001b) have yet to reappear.[2] Taken as a whole, these poems demonstrate both familiar and newly surprising aspects of Duncan Bush's writing, especially in how they resemble some of those in an earlier 'Anglo-Welsh' canon.

Notes

1 Any dates for the uncollected poems refer to their magazine or journal publication.

2 'Death Will Come and It Will Have Your Eyes', 'You, Wind of March', 'I Shall Go Through the Piazza di Spagna', 'The Night You Slept' and 'The Cats Will Know'.

15

Screen life (including unpublished, undated writings)

Duncan Bush was an excellent choice to present *Voices in the Dark: One Hundred Years of Cinema in Wales* for BBC Wales/Cymru television. The programme was directed by Steve Freer and screened in 1997. But, as Duncan Bush writes of his own childhood: 'Television came late to the Bush household. I think I must have been one of the last in my class at school to watch tv on a daily basis' (from his unpublished and undated papers). Undoubtedly, film, television and comics supplied Bush with a consistent source of imagery until his death, and he deliberately developed a cinematic imagination. His favourite programme for family viewing was *Z-Cars*, from the BBC, early in the 1960s. In those same writings, he notes appreciatively:

> *Z-Cars* was to run for many years, but none of the subsequent episodes had the impact of that first 6-part series . . . not only the groundbreaking originality and radicalism of John McGrath's scripts and a strong ensemble cast of largely understated actors but the peculiar immediacy which the Armchair Theatre plays [on ITV] also had: that unmistakable intensity – which is somehow communicated without the audience at home ever realizing what causes it – of drama televised 'live'.

The power of *Z-Cars* remains alive as I write this in 2024. Its familiar theme tune (performed by Johnny Keating) is played at every home match for Everton football club, at Goodison Park, Liverpool. This is the same theme music with which Bush would have been familiar.

Much of his writing had already revealed his love of screen culture, whether on television or film. This is Bush writing in prolonged haiku-form. The poem is titled 'The Eden of the Suburbs' and is part of his 'Hollywood Wildlife' series:

Have we lived here once? Only
By proxy – before

Imagination's
Exile to a world denser
Than films yet orphaned

To memories vivid,
Secondhand as dreams: the lost
Adulthoods we grieve.

(2007b)

In the 'All the Scattered Fragments' section of *The Genre of Silence*, we learn:

The broken plate won't

fly back together again
or the dead get

smartly up off the floor
like gymnasts, in that

magical way things happen
in a film rewinding.

(1988b)

That word 'magical' suggests some form of enchantment. Might film triumph over death? And these are the last words of the novel. This is a similar image to that which concludes 'And Suddenly it's Evening', as the dead in the old man's memory 'throw back the turf' (1997a) (see chapter 9).

But the inundation by film of Bush's work is especially true of *Glass Shot* and *Now All the Rage*, in which the focal character, Guy, lectures on film, as did Bush in Newport.

In an unpublished and undated essay/memoir, some of which in terms of imagery has been used, or was possibly earmarked for use, in poetry, Bush writes:

> When we lived in Llandaff North, we went to the Tivoli, a few hundred yards down the road from our flat, and opposite the Tizer factory; then, after we moved to Coryton [now north Cardiff], we had a choice of two local picture houses within walking distance: the Monico in Rhiwbina – one of the more middle-class suburbs of the city – and the Rialto in Old Church Road, Whitchurch. The 'Ri' was a squalid, run-down building, with torn seats and fetid lavatories (the 'Gents' was little more than a slab of slate with a blocked trough at its foot in which cigarette-ends disintegrated . . .).

He adds:

> Very occasionally, however, we'd catch a bus to the Plaza in Gabalfa, a large, well-appointed cinema with a screen wide enough for CinemaScope, where the 'big' films seemed to come first. I think we saw *The Bridge on the River Kwai* (1957) there.
>
> . . .
>
> Monico, Rialto, Tivoli, Plaza . . . Why the fashion for Mediterranean names? It suggests a modern variety of the piazza or pleasure garden, the mingling ground of a crowd democratised by a thirst for entertainment – now brought indoors.

In another fragment from his unpublished papers, Bush writes: 'My father always called the Rialto "The Bomb and Dagger" – a term from the early days of silent melodramas, but in recognition of its fleapit shabbiness.' In this text, Bush admits that he did find certain British war films 'celebrating national heroism' enjoyable, despite the officers' and soldiers' clear class demarcations. These included *The Cruel Sea* (1953), *The Dam Busters* (1955), *Reach for the Sky* and *The Man Who Never Was* (1956), and *Carve Her Name with Pride* (1958). However, he also writes, in his undated papers:

> I also remember hard-edged modern American dramas like *The Big Heat* [1953] and *On the Waterfront* (1954). These made British silly-ass film comedies, such as *Genevieve* (1953) and *Doctor in the House* (1954) seem old hat even to a seven- or eight-year-old. And the cynicism and sense of classlessness one absorbed from these tough-guy movies contributed to the post-war British craze for American culture.

This section of the unpublished 'screen life' writing has individual sections devoted to 'heroes' and 'a heroine'. Frankie Laine, the singer, is named 'First' hero. 'Second' is Gilbert Roland, the Mexican actor:

> handsome in a raddled way and beautifully dressed throughout with the slight ostentation appropriate to an ageing heart-throb, for me he steals every scene he appears in. One entrance with a pure white cashmere overcoat draped across his shoulders (that is, without his arms in the sleeves) has always represented to me the quintessence of negligent elegance which is the true definition of style.

The 'Third' hero is actor, Robert Ryan, 'another film star who was never a leading man'; while 'A Heroine' is Grace Kelly. Indeed, Bush writes a good deal about Kelly:

> And what I, as an eight- or nine-year-old boy, fell for in Grace Kelly was probably not just her beauty but a tomboy quality I've always been drawn to in women, and which can be divined beneath her ineffable sophistication. She was never anything but a brick and a good egg.

Films made Bush want to write. In 'Going to the Pictures in the Fifties' he tells us:

> I fell in love with Rhonda Fleming
> In Inferno. But then I saw
> Natalie Wood in The Searchers –
>
> At the end of which, like J.-L. Goddard,
> I even loved John Wayne.
>
> (1997a)

But he was particularly stricken by Grace Kelly: 'Grace Kelly's looks are still classically elegant, still mysteriously erotic. No-one was better on Kodak, her beauty is as potent as ever on film and in photographs, and completely contemporary.' And this, from his unpublished comments on her film *Dial M for Murder*: 'Probably when I saw the film I was simply entranced by her loveliness and her clear cut-glass English accent, just as I was excited by her sense of fun and her driving-style'.

It must be his own reading he references here when he surmises:

> Grace's promiscuity is legendary, even in Hollywood. But when you read in the scandal-sheet biographies about her affairs . . . what strikes you is not only her sexual readiness . . . an emotional enthusiasm which seems a form of purity rather than the contrary
>
> . . .
>
> Every time in later years when I happened to be in France and I picked up a Paris Match at a newsagents and read about another scandal involving her beautiful, headstrong daughters, what invariably touched me was not the sad and profligate dramas that rich, spoiled women are capable of causing in the absence of firm, maternal control . . .

For me, this says as much about Bush as it does his subject. Duncan Bush admired style – see 'West 86th Street' in *The Flying Trapeze*, the 2023 version of 'Robert Lowell', and his unpublished writing about his mother's dressing-table in the undated 'Pond's Cold Cream', an extract of which appears in the next chapter of this volume.

In his discussion of (Princess) Grace Kelly, Bush is able to apply the adjective 'anuran' (resembling a tail-less amphibian) to film director Alfred Hitchcock. Another 'unusual' word ticked off. All of these heroes I imagine, were developed when Bush attended Whitchurch Grammar School in north Cardiff, from the late 1950s. Duncan Bush admired those films and film stars because of the obvious craft and dedication of the film-makers and actors themselves. His work as a lecturer in Newport, and all his writings, attest to this. Always he understands the powerful effect that film and acting technique can have on an audience. Throughout his life, Bush himself was a critical but enthusiastic part of that audience.

16

Short prose (including unpublished work)

Short stories

This chapter discusses a range of prose writing. Short stories by Duncan Bush were published irregularly, and it was my assumption that Bush considered the short story of lesser importance than poetry or the novel. For me, many of his poems were short stories in themselves, especially those in *Masks* (1994) and *Midway* (1997).

The first that readers encountered was 'Boss' (1986). Its imagery chimes with that of Bush's poetry, especially 'European Capital', where:

> These Brussels burghers swim like slow fish
> In their long café aquariums. My dream, too,
> Is long, silt-heavy as the Congo.
>
> (1994a)

The main character in 'Boss' is a resourceful woman who has to exist in a hateful system, her body her only resource: 'At one point she took the coarse, close-curled Afro wig out of the box and – cigarette in mouth, squinting against the smoke – fitted it carefully over her skull, turning her head from side to side to judge the effect in the dressing-table mirror' (1986a). This unnamed woman may be white. Yet she prepares for each sexual rendezvous by blackening her skin, a luxurious process, and Bush takes time in describing the process: 'The woman was tall, and perhaps too thin. But these were doubts to which she'd almost ceased to give credibility. Height was important for a model. And as to thinness, well thinness was the only grace there was' (1986a). She relates the behaviour of one of her clients. From my reading I take this man to be white Afrikaans. She will encourage him to talk:

> As for the stories themselves, though – well they were straight out of the comics, or those old Tarzan films . . . He trapped black panthers with a tethered goat. He shot the heads clean off deadly snakes . . . In other words he lived in some preternatural bush from which, at evening, he returned – a place teeming like a film poster, with a different danger or adventure in each corner of the layout. (1986a)

Apart from the political and social thrust of 'Boss', I don't find Duncan Bush's short stories essential. Characters or situations described are sketched but not developed. Indeed, characters within the poetry can appear better formed, as is the cast of 'European Capital', in *Masks*.

'The Snowy Owl', which, Bush's biographical note informs us, is from 'a novel in progress', is found in the anthology *Drawing Down the Moon*. Here, as in his poetry, Duncan Bush is careful in his description of the bird: 'It must have stood over a foot tall on its perch . . . It had big yellow eyes. The feathers were pure white, with a big sooty-brown mark in them like ermine, but more like a barring. It had furred claws' (1995c). Seren Books have verbally communicated to myself (early 2023) about the existence of either a novel or an idea for such, subsequent to *Glass Shot* (1991), apparently centred on south Powys, that contains owl imagery. And there are similarities in terms of location with the poem 'Down on Britains Farm' (*Midway*), with its reference to 'the brother of a neighbour of a man I know in Mynydd Epynt' (1997a).

'An Evening with your Ex' was published in *Tilting at Windmills* (1995). This also contains avian imagery. Speaking of the women in his life, the leading male character states: 'Peacocks or bower birds they're not. The mating display and the big tease can be hard to tell apart' (1995a). It's also possible to read chapter 8 from *Glass Shot* as an individual story, such is its seeming discrete existence.

Alun Richards ensured Bush was represented in *The Second Penguin Book of Welsh Short Stories*, but, maybe surprisingly, Dai Smith, who lavished praise on Allan Bush's only novel, selected nothing by Duncan for the two-volume *Story: The Library of Wales Short Story Anthology*.

'Lavernock' and other unpublished prose

In a published essay by Duncan Bush titled 'The Sea, The Sea', commissioned by Cary Archard and J. P. Ward for *Poetry Wales*, he writes of St Donat's, near Llantwit Major, 'where my wife teaches English and, until recently, I too taught part-time' (1985c). The overall title for the series of which 'The Sea, The Sea' is a part is 'Places', and it is Lavernock, a seaside location once reachable by Duncan himself from Cardiff, that Bush most clearly depicts, 'not overcrowded, crass, commercialized, expensive Barry'.

The essay is explicit:

> when my wife and small son and I came back to South Wales, to St Donat's, in the summer of 1982, I saw what was still here . . . those eroding grey-and-yellow limestone cliffs barred horizontally with strata, like the breast of the honey-buzzard in the birdbook. I was thirty-five years old – half the biblical span: and felt it had taken all of that for those cliffs to show through in me; as a rock formation wears through topsoil . . . Perhaps writing, like electricity, sometimes needs to be earthed.

Honey-buzzard; peacock; bower bird; barn owl; snowy owl; shrikes ('Shrikes at Jaulny'); hobby ('To the Hawk, Fallen'). When Bush depicts birds they are UK rarities or 'exotic'.

'The Sea, The Sea' may have been the result of literary distillation when Bush was compiling his 'A Sense of Place' writings. Amongst copies of Duncan Bush's papers given to me in January, 2021 by Annette Weaver, was a prose work titled 'Lavernock'. This might be part of a memoir, or even an autobiography, or 'notes' towards either. I have quoted from this work in chapter 2. References to 'Lavernock', and his attraction to that 'muddy, sometimes smelly beach on the coast west of Cardiff, just around the headland from Penarth', appeared throughout his life, including in the play *Sailing to America* and the novel *Glass Shot*.

Of the prose writings presented to me by Annette Weaver, I find 'Lavernock' the most significant, because of the sense of completion. It begins in typical style. Bush again agrees he is part of the Celtic diaspora, subject to the disease (or hypochondria) of homesickness. But he refuses to use the Welsh-language form *hiraeth*, which provides a particular word for this longing. In 'Lavernock', he combines social with personal detail, presenting a historic picture:

> This was the middle Fifties: the halcyon days before diesel trains, before Beeching. They were compartment trains, without corridors, and the seats of rough blue Wilton fabric had a peppery reek of ancient dust. Above them were luggage racks of netted cord, like hammocks, and a foxed mirror between sempiternally sunny scenes of Great Yarmouth or the Wye at Symond's Yat. To lower the window you tugged, then released, a leather belt like a razor strop: and when you thrust out your abruptly wind-shocked head . . .

In the same fragment, he writes about arrival at Lavernock, which:

> was the beach Cardiff people went to on summer Sundays in my boyhood, and, as I wrote in the ringing prose I aimed for . . . If I was nostalgic for it in later life it was because an exile dreams of returning not only to 'a mythic landscape', but 'in quest for some former self, 'a golden age' . . .

To which Bush adds: 'Overwritten or not, this was true and still is.'

> Lavernock was those early Sunday mornings in summer, still cool before the heat, and a press of families standing on the platform at Llandaff North station waiting for a train that was already half full and would be packed to standing-room only by the time it left Grangetown [Stew Boyle country] two stops later.

It's possible to see Duncan Bush as a kind of class-exile. His 'Wales' was Lavernock and north Llandaff, and because of this he celebrated them with evocative writing. Yet he understood they were irrecoverable.

'Lavernock' leads on to prose pieces with titles such as 'Severn' and 'Relocate', all of which might have been used in future writings. These might even be sections of a more ambitious 'Lavernock'. Another fragment sees Bush describing 'Cory Hall' in north Cardiff:

> Like every modern suburb, Coryton had been countryside not long before – rural enough, at least around the turn of the century, for a member of the ship-owning and coal-exporting Cory family to have built Cory Hall there, a handsome red brick mansion in extensive wooded grounds. It had been requisitioned by the Army during the war, and lay derelict throughout the Fifties and Sixties. In my early teenage years a gang of us sometimes trespassed in the grounds.

It is difficult to imagine Bush not using such material for future poetry.

Another of the unpublished prose pieces is titled 'Pond's Cold Cream', in which the mature Duncan lists what the young Duncan 'found on my mother's dressing table'. This is worth quoting at greater length:

> Pond's Cold Cream came in a little jar of opaque white glass, and Coty rouge in a tiny flat circular box, like a snuff-box – I like this particularly, for its dark-blue colour and tight-fitting lid which bore the single word 'Coty': it was the foreign-sounding name, the elegant simplicity of its lettering and perhaps the patrician confidence that a name alone is enough to sell a product which impressed me – as they often still do – as a guarantee of quality, and a pinnacle of the advertiser's craft.

(See also 'Douce France' in *The Flying Trapeze* for that love of blue colours.)

In 'Pond's Cold Cream', Duncan notes that Californian Poppy was the name of his mother's favourite perfume. He has a memory of 'unscrewing the bottle and sniffing the contents'. Then, accidentally, spilling a little over himself. 'Did this really happen? Or did I just invent it, as I might have with an incident in a novel?' This is similar to the unpublished description of Bush hiding in a clothes basket when playing with a friend, quoted in chapter 8. Unsurprisingly, there are places where he quotes himself from past writings. Not only was genre fluid, but texts themselves were to be constantly refined and made adaptable.

'Scrapbooks' (unpublished), is an account of putting together a 'scrapbook' and then looking at it years later. Bush writes:

> What's the erotic or emotional significance of a photograph of Hedy Lamarr or Clark Gable? . . . These are secrets a diary might tell us, but in the scrapbook we have only the objective testimony of the photograph. These items are evidence – but of what?

Lamarr, Gable, Pond's Cold Cream, Coty rouge, Californian Poppy perfume: all such names (like 'Kuchiouk-Hanem' in the poem 'Gill (1970)', see chapter 9) are particularities that place an image in the reader's imagination.

In the unpublished work 'Interview at Atlantic College', Bush writes of the interview he and Annette Weaver shared for positions at Atlantic College, near St Donat's, Llantwit Major, south Wales, Annette as a prospective English teacher, while Duncan would 'be expected to play an enthusiastic supporting role in the life of the College'. For the (successful) interview, the couple brought along the one-year-old Joe Bush.

Bush also writes about homecoming, and not merely concerning 'the anxieties of being a second-home owner. The absentee.' (Who might say whether he considered the Meibion Glyndŵr campaign of burning second homes a threat to his eventual house in Ynyswen

– purchased 1984 – where Welsh is commonly spoken? Annette Weaver told me on 24 November, 2024 that she had intended learning Welsh before Duncan's death.)

The following is from the provisionally titled work 'Severn':

> But what I love is the Heraclitean changeableness of this magnificent, reversible river: the fact that one day when I cross it the immense estuary will be a wrinkled, brownish sea, full as a brimming bowl, and next time a glittering delta of brief archipelagoes, black with seaweed.

Other unpublished writings are illuminative. 'Praise' has Bush commenting on his early success as a reader, and being able to make everything a 'performance' that might earn him the encouragement he craved. Yes, he implies, he was 'successful' with the spoken word, and he then provides lists of the words he one day hoped would appear in his writings. See also *Now All the Rage* (see chapter 12 above), and his essay 'Abecedarian to Shagtastic' for further comments, like this:

> Yet I've always maintained a scepticism about language too, and an abiding sense of its privacy; and, at the cost of seeming to agree with that sesquipedalian charlatan Derrida, a deep sense of the primacy of the written word – the word discovered and articulated in silence – is behind the fact that I've always mistrusted spoken language, and distrusted individuals who are too loquacious or prompt to self-account: those plausible talkers who have all the instincts of compulsive liars. (2003a)

This may be the reason why Duncan Bush was drawn to creating literary personae. He uses some of this in a fragmentary memoir of his father, contained within the unpublished papers: 'This is the fate of all raconteurs and bar-counter wits, all compulsive anecdotalists and self-mythologisers . . . a remorseless standardization of the stories themselves.' He has in mind both writers, returning to established themes, and performers, of the spoken-word variety, here. Duncan Bush did reuse his own particular favourite words, 'paravail' and 'atavistic' especially.

And finally, this a fragment that links Bush's memories concerned with this part of the Welsh coast, and his life in England:

> It was in the summer of 1982, and I was thirty-six. I was recently married, and we had a year-old son. After the wedding – which took place in that haven of secularity, Gravesend Registry Office – I announced to the guests that Annette and I were marrying . . . because there were tax advantages in matrimony as a legal state which we chose not to forego.
>
> I thought this a gallant and original declaration of radical credentials . . . and all it does now is prove that I was no different from a million other grant-educated prigs who'd learned their political philosophy in the heady purisms of the 1960s and '70s.

Maybe this is a fragment of autobiography or even a sketch for a larger work. Amongst other unpublished papers, Duncan Bush writes more about his father (see chapter 2).

17

Other writings and reviews

Duncan Bush supported certain writers whose work he approved, and he reviewed them in magazines he found sympathetic. These included *Poetry Wales*, *Luxemburger Wort* and the *London Magazine*. This last proved a good friend to Bush: between 2001 and 2007 he contributed an essay, 'Adlestrop Revisited' (2001), and a series of ten reviews, demonstrating wide literary interests. These included two Ian McEwan novels, *Saturday* (reviewed in 2005) and *On Chesil Beach* (2007). His reviews contain familiar Bush subjects: photography and travel, in a review of *Wilfred Thesiger: A Life in Pictures* (2005); film, in a review of *Nobody's Perfect: Billy Wilder, A Personal Biography*, by Charlotte Chandler (2003); exile, a review of Elias Canetti's *Party in the Blitz* (2006); and French literature, *Voltaire Almighty* by Roger Pearson, and *Monsieur Proust* by Celeste Albaret (2004).

Probably Bush was familiar with the Dannie Abse poem 'Not Adlestrop' (1977), but his essay in the *London Magazine* is similar to his writing and translation of Cesar Pavese in the *Amsterdam Review*, in the way his 'fictionalizing imagination' creates a portrait of what appears to be a real person encountered by Bush, visiting Adlestrop: 'He looked at me with a kind of benign slyness. He had a pink, smooth face; and hazel eyes which you saw had not changed since he was a boy' (2001). This man is similar to the hotelier in the Hotel Roma in Turin, described by Duncan Bush in the *Amsterdam Review* (2004; see chapter 11), both credible, created by a few brushstrokes. The essay also contains another familiar concern:

> It's too easy to draw analogies which don't exist between modern poetry and photography (in the way writers in the nineteenth century made comparisons between poetry and music or sculpture). But there's a kind of poetry which records what Henri Cartier-Bresson, a photographer, famously called 'the Decisive Moment'. Or which recognizes that certain moments are decisive. (2001)

As his editor I found that Bush agreed only to commissions to review books he considered worthwhile. His words on the American poet Stephen Dobyns contain typical phraseology: 'Dobyns is above all fascinated by the irreal "where the fantastic (has) become a commonplace"' (1998). And I have no doubt that it was Bush himself who suggested he review Canetti, intrigued by his cosmopolitanism and self-exiled life. Once more, that assertion in his essay 'North-East of Eden' that 'exile is a powerful force for the imagination' might apply (2002b).

In the *London Magazine*, Bush reviewed *Saturday*, by Ian McEwan, a novel concerning one day in the life of Henry Perowne, a neurosurgeon, who lives in a 'perfect' Regency square in London. The Saturday in question is the day of the demonstration against the 2003 Iraq war, which reportedly saw the largest crowd of people ever assembled in the capital. 'That serious writers are able to move into higher and higher Council Tax bands may reflect well on contemporary culture in Britain . . . The risk is that a writer's work suffers a gradual, irreversible process of gentrification, like Islington'. Although Bush is aware of McEwan's possible satire in his portrait of Perowne, nevertheless he writes that:

> Saturday will lay bare not only the recondite professional knowledge as a neurologist but his prowess at squash and his skill in making a fish stew. This last stands as telling symbol of a universalizing middle-class culture, whereby the traditions of French peasant cuisine become fashionable commonplaces by way of the supplements of English Sunday newspapers. (2005a)

He concludes: 'This is a gripping novel, in which the world of the Perownes is threatened by a savagery which their own affluence itself seems almost to provoke.' Bush, already the author of 'Navvies' and *Glass Shot*, and who did not share ownership of property until aged almost forty, finds '*Saturday* a compelling contemporary novel, with all the mounting tension of a thriller' (2005a).

Annette Weaver writes to me of other Duncan Bush writings that appeared in English in a Luxembourg publication, of which many of his UK readers might have been oblivious. She says:

> Between approximately 1999 and 2013 Duncan was a regular contributor of book reviews to the *Luxemburger Wort*, the main and oldest daily newspaper in Luxembourg (to give the alternative French spelling of the Grand Duchy). Originally in German, it was/is a bilingual publication also known as *La Voix*. Like the country the paper is European in its openness to languages, and produced a weekly arts and literature supplement, *Die Warte*, with reviews in German, French, Lëtzebuergesch and English, the first three being official national languages and the latter a de facto one.
>
> As a European who relished language in all its forms, Duncan was happy to contribute, especially as it provided him with English-language books he would otherwise have had to wait to read. With a largely free choice, occasionally based around a theme, his selection of subjects to review was eclectic, from novels and biographies to anthologies and journalism. This allowed him to follow up on some old favourites, such as the selected and collected works of Cyril Connolly and George Orwell or the biography of Billy Wilder and autobiography of Simon Gray.
>
> Fiction ranged from William Boyd and Julia Blackburn to Jed Mercurio and Raymond Briggs. Duncan enjoyed the exercise of writing under journalistic constraints and the opportunity to hone his always-critical faculties on a defined target. The reviews provide a counterweight to some of his later poetry in that they were almost wholly positive, evidence of his move in later life towards what he described in his Orwell piece as 'the humanism of experience'. (pers. corr. 2024)

There exist over forty of these *Luxemburger Wort* reviews. As with his ambitions for the *Amsterdam Review*, for me they reveal Bush as a writer determined to compound his European credentials.

Also, for *Granta*, he wrote the essay 'Claudia Cardinale is a Mexican Revolutionary', which begins with a jibe at 'sofa-slugs' (see 'The

Calais Caricatures', quoted in chapter 14). The essay reveals Bush again fascinated by screen figures:

> Claudia Cardinale is a Mexican revolutionary. Not that you know that straight away . . .
>
> Lee Marvin is an armaments expert and Burt Lancaster a dynamiter . . . both drifters, desperadoes, mercenaries awash from their last professional war . . .
>
> Burt Lancaster is . . . a rough diamond and something of a womanizer . . . Sounds corny when you try to write it down, and perhaps it is. But I've always liked Lancaster's style. (1983)

That word 'style' again. And by now, we understand what it means to Bush and also its 'corny' possibilities. And 'desperadoes', used by Bush in his description of his father's wartime stories. Even looking ahead, Bush was never estranged from his past.

18

Afterword

Determinedly cosmopolitan, a European citizen of the world – (see all his published writings, but particularly his review/essay 'North-East of Eden' (2002b)) – and always an ambitiously experimental writer, Duncan Bush set the bar high for himself. Perhaps in Wales we are not used to writers attempting that.

From 'Lash LaRue and the River of Adventure' (*Midway*), I read: 'Looking back now, it seems inevitable that he [I] would try to be an actor or a writer: one of those auto-fantasists who become the compulsive fabricators of other selves' (1997a). Also, Duncan Bush was able to state, in an interview with Richard Poole: 'I'm committed to the rather un-British idea of the writer as intellectual (rather than mere "wordsmith"). And writers have to be prepared to take sides'. Bush knew what side his whole sensibility told him to support during and after the UK miners' strike of 1984/5. And I find this crucial, from the same interview with Richard Poole:

> Good writing is political in the widest sense, rather than the narrower, factional senses. Writers have commitments, like every other citizen. But it shouldn't be the group or party line – the political version of the Received Idea – which emerges in their work.
>
> I actually think that the noblest role for a writer is that of the eternal renegade or maverick; that annoying, irritating, frequently resented presence – the complete antithesis of the 'group mentality'.
>
> Like all Celts I've always been grateful for not being English – and this, which might imply if not an aesthetic, then at least a rejection of

> metropolitan literary fashions – has perhaps been more important than I realize. (Poole, 1992a)

Many other people on these islands, and they do not have to be 'Celts', are either alienated by 'metropolitan literary fashions' or are oblivious of such. With his use of 'maverick', Bush echoes John Tripp, for whom he wrote the Welsh Union of Writers obituary in 1986. Tripp had written that he responded best to any writer whom he considered 'a gifted exploding maverick' (Jenkins, 1989). And that is how John Tripp considered himself – a romanticised idea of the English-language poet in Wales.

Linked to this is Bush's insistence on a fluidity of form being an option he worked to create for himself, and which he admired in other writers:

> poetry doesn't have to be laid out any particular way at all. In other words I'm not sure what the differences (between prose and poetry are) anymore. Any more than I know why or how one idea leads to a poem, or a sequence of poems, and another leads to a story or eventually a novel. (Poole, 1992a)

Poole's decision to base almost a special issue of *Poetry Wales* on Bush (his first issue, by the way, and including his own important essay, 'Duncan Bush's Personae') should be applauded. Poole justifies this because 'this writer has refused that limiting self-consciousness', which has exerted too strong a stranglehold on 'Anglo-Welsh' writing. In this essay Poole writes:

> the cultivation of persona signifies the poet's desire to encompass modes of being and kinds of experience that are not and could never be his or her own. The persona is put on like a garment, a sensibility not the poet's own is worn like a mask of many colours . . . Now, instead of a tension between the claims of the poet and the requirements of the poem, we get a tension between the sensibility of the poet and the sensibility of the persona. (Poole, 1992b)

M. Wynn Thomas has described the subject of this volume in his *Corresponding Cultures*:

> Bush . . . is a child of the 1950s, his America discovered through the glamour of Hollywood cinema, brash Yankee comics, Frankie Laine records on old 78s, and other seductive images of energy and abundance vividly superimposed on the drabness of an exhausted, belt-tightening post-war Britain. (1999)

Duncan identifies with 'working-class culture', as in the best of *Z-Cars*, but has exacting standards. Another fragment, undated, has him describing himself 'born into a working class family on the northern edge of Cardiff'. But he preferred to use the word 'demotic' for descriptions of the language of some of his works (the online thesaurus has these synonyms for 'demotic': conversational, vernacular, chatty, common, dialectal and everyday). Duncan Bush never forgot his origins in 'rented rooms' and for how long such rooms were part of his life. Certainly this was a fact that helped him compose *Glass Shot* and 'Are There Still Wolves in Pennsylvania?', and even *Now All the Rage*, in which Guy Hughes would appear to be attempting to leave any 'working class' associations behind.

I reiterate the words of Phil Cope of Valley and Vale Community Arts in Bridgend (in chapter 4) about how much he appreciated Bush's 'powerful, gritty and insightful language' on the community projects they shared. The 'sense of classlessness' that Bush writes about in his undated papers, having been absorbed from American 'hard-edged' films of the 1950s, I find very much linked to his politics, his class-identification, and independence of spirit.

Duncan Bush was a writer always alert to acting techniques (I look again at the original cover of *Midway*, where Bush himself seems to peer over the two actors' shoulders). While at Oxford, he took part in staged drama. We should recall, as Christine Pagnoulle (1995) does, that Duncan acted in his own play – *Cocktails for Three*, staged in Oxford, in 1970. Performance was vital to him. By this, I mean in film, theatre, television. As to 'unmistakable intensity', Bush's best writings are full of it, as the poet combines all the languages available to him, demotic and academic. Plus his (sometimes) ironically used 'unusual' words.

In a letter to me, Ian Gregson has written:

> Although Duncan Bush died in 2017, his work retains its relevance in the 2020s because of its sceptical exploration of identity politics. His Welshness is always at least implicit in his work (he was born in Cardiff in 1946) but he lived most of his adult life in Luxembourg, and he poured scorn on national feeling and dismissed Wales 'as a topic which interests only the Welsh, and by no means all of them'.

As I have stated in chapter 5, I do not believe it accurate to state that Duncan Bush 'dismissed Wales'. But Gregson continues: 'His angry rejection of nationalisms, especially those of Wales and England, has acquired, since Brexit, a more chilling topicality since his death, and his damning verdict on English patriots, "who love the pound and hate 'asylum-seekers'" is now a much more urgent diagnosis' (pers. corr. 2023).

M. Wynn Thomas is astute in locating the origins of Bush's sensibility 'in his angry identification with the class-ridden, ethnically divided West Britain (south Wales) of his childhood and youth in the Llandaff area of Cardiff' (1999): however, Bush strenuously evolved a poetic which drew upon that angry identification to explore what the combination of class and ethnicity mean internationally.

Bush's writing is extremely wide-ranging, from an early stage introducing 'persona' poems, such as 'Pneumoconiosis' (1973), which is emblematic of his identification with workers and the working class, and including references to gardening, history (both remote and recent), ornithology, politics, Wales and places beyond Wales, especially England, France, Luxembourg, Italy, Germany, Russia, the USA, Kenya, Australia, Palestine and South Africa, and photography and film.

His writing is able to demonstrate both humanitarian empathy and (sometimes) edgy satire, much of it born out of his particularising and cinematic imagination, and his organic ability to create credible personae, the most powerful being Victor Bal and the terrifying Stew Boyle. Regarding the latter, *Glass Shot* consists of relentless male sexual fantasy, of a type that many people find distasteful. As we have seen in the chapter devoted to the novel, there is a groundswell of opinion that deems publication of such work should not occur.

Bush's translations and 'versions' reveal his ambition – they include Baudelaire, Montale, Mallarmé, Pasolini and Cesare Pavese. He relied on his linguistic facility and literary curiosity to create and enrich his own poetry.

Intrigued and appalled by what modern concepts of fame and literary celebrity have come to mean, Bush used his readings of writers such as Basil Bunting and, more tragically, Cesare Pavese to balance the scales in what he believed an unhealthy quest. Bunting lived what Bush might have considered an 'honourable' writer's life. For Pavese, literary fame was meaningless without a significant human relationship.

Duncan Bush died in 2017, fighting cancer for his final five years. What characterised this writer, both at the end of his life and its beginning, was his scrupulous ambition, linked with a determination not to compromise with either fashion or taste.

In the near future I trust a new volume of uncollected and previously unpublished material by Duncan Bush might appear, and thus be made available to new and existing readers. I am also mindful that no selected or collected volume of his published poetry or other writings is currently available. Finally, I concur with Sam Adams (2023), who states that 'Duncan Bush has had nothing like the wider recognition that his writing has consistently merited'.

Bibliography

Works by Duncan Bush

Bush, D. (1973), 'Pneumoconiosis', *Poetry Wales*, 9/3.

Bush, D. (1980), *Nostos* (Swansea: Swansea Poetry Workshop).

Bush, D. (1982), translations of Cesar Pavese, 'Agony' and 'Those Who Were There', *Poetry Wales*,18/2.

Bush, D. (1983), 'Claudia Cardinale is a Mexican Revolutionary', in *Granta 8: Dirty Realism* (Granta Magazine). Available at: *https://granta.com/claudia-cardinale-is-a-mexican-revolutionary/* Accessed September 2023.

Bush, D. (1984), *Aquarium* (Bridgend: Seren).

Bush, D. (1985a), *Black Faces, Red Mouths* (Ynyswen: Bedrock Press).

Bush, D. (1985b), 'The Last Room: Chabra Camp 1983', *Poetry Wales*, 21/1.

Bush, D. (1985c), 'The Sea, The Sea', *Poetry Wales*, 21/1.

Bush, D. (1986a), 'Boss', 'Crocuses' and 'White Sugar', in M. Elfyn and N. Jenkins (eds), *Poets Against Apartheid / Beirdd yn Erbyn Apartheid* (Cardiff: Wales Anti-Apartheid Movement).

Bush, D. (1986b) (ed.), *On Censorship* (Cardiff: Welsh Union of Writers).

Bush, D. (1986c), *Salt* (Bridgend: Seren).

Bush, D. (1987), 'Foreword: Portrait of an Artist', in S. Smith, *Picture: Welsh Poets* (Bridgend: Seren).

Bush, D. (1988a), 'Bardot in Grangetown', *Poetry Wales*, 24/2.

Bush, D. (1988b), *The Genre of Silence* (Bridgend: Seren).

Bush, D. (1989), Welsh Union of Writers obituary of John Tripp, quoted in N. Jenkins, *John Tripp: Writers of Wales* (Cardiff: University of Wales Press).

Bush, D. (1991), *Glass Shot* (London: Secker and Warburg; 1993 pbk edn, Mandarin).

Bush, D. (1994a), *Masks* (Bridgend: Seren).
Bush, D. (1994b), 'The Last Thrush', in A. Richards (ed.), *The Second Penguin Book of Welsh Short Stories* (Harmondsworth: Penguin).
Bush, D. (1995a), 'An Evening with Your Ex', in R. Pawar (ed.), *Tilting at Windmills, New Welsh Short Fiction* (Cardigan: Parthian).
Bush, D. (1995b), 'Pneumoconiosis', poster with artist Wil Rowlands (Cardiff: Arts Council of Wales).
Bush, D. (1995c), 'The Snowy Owl', in R. Minhinnick (ed.), *Drawing Down the Moon* (Bridgend: Seren).
Bush, D. (1997a), *Midway* (Bridgend: Seren).
Bush, D. (1997b), *Sailing to America*, in P. Clark (ed.), *Act One Wales: Thirteen One Act Plays* (Bridgend: Seren).
Bush, D. (1997c), *The Hook* (Bridgend: Seren).
Bush, D. (1998), review of Stephen Dobyns, two poetry collections, *Poetry Wales*, 33/4.
Bush, D. (2001a), 'Adlestrop Revisited', *The London Magazine*, December–January.
Bush, D. (2001b), five versions of Pavese, 'Death Will Come and It Will Have Your Eyes', 'You, Wind of March', 'I Shall Go Through the Piazza di Spagna', 'The Night You Slept' and 'The Cats Will Know', *Poetry Wales*, 37/1.
Bush, D. (2002a), 'Francophilia', *Poetry Wales*, 37/4.
Bush, D. (2002b), 'North-East of Eden', *Poetry Wales*, 38/1.
Bush, D. (2002c), 'On Matthew Arnold and Pastoral', *Poetry Wales*, 38/3.
Bush, D. (2003a), 'Abecedarian to Shagtastic', *Poetry Wales*, 39/3.
Bush, D. (2003b), 'At St Mary Redcliffe', *Poetry Wales*, 39/2.
Bush, D. (2003c), 'The Wilder side', review of Charlotte Chandler, *Billy Wilder: A Personal Biography*, *The London Magazine*, October–November.
Bush, D. (2004a), translations from Cesar Pavese, 'Death Will Come and It Will Have Your Eyes', *The Amsterdam Review*, 1.
Bush, D. (2004b), translation from Pavese, 'The Cats Will Know', *The Amsterdam Review*, 1.
Bush, D. (2004c), 'Unparalleled intimacy', review of Celeste Albaret, *Monsieur Proust*, trans. B. Bray, *The London Magazine*, August–September.
Bush, D. (2004d) (as Jay McGill), 'Paragliding and the Art of Serious Fiction', *The Amsterdam Review*, 1.
Bush, D. (2005a), 'A life in the day', review of Ian McEwan, *Saturday*, *The London Magazine*, June–July.

Bush, D. (2005b), 'Paris Haikus' and 'At Giverny', *Poetry Wales*, 41/1.

Bush, D. (2005c) (as Jay McGill), 'Sebald's Itineraries', *The Amsterdam Review*, 2.

Bush, D. (2005d) (as Jay McGill), 'Avedon's Drifters', *The Amsterdam Review*, 2.

Bush, D. (2005e) (as Pierre de La Prée), 'Poem at Eleven O'Clock', 'A Season in Sarajevo', 'Douce France', *The Amsterdam Review*, 2.

Bush, D. (2006a), 'In an exile's eye', review of Elias Canetti, *Party in the Blitz*, trans. M. Hofmann, *The London Magazine*, February–March.

Bush, D. (2006b), 'A life of Voltaire', review of Roger Pearson, *Voltaire Almighty*, *The London Magazine*, June–July.

Bush, D. (2007a), *Now All the Rage* (Exeter: Colophon Books).

Bush, D. (2007b), 'Hollywood Wildlife', *Poetry Wales*, 43/1.

Bush, D. (2007c), 'Sedimentological dynamics', review of Ian McEwan, *On Chesil Beach*, *The London Magazine*, August–September.

Bush, D. (2010), 'The Mexican Border at Night', *Poetry Wales*, 45/4.

Bush, D. (2012a), 'Hay Festival', online (unavailable), Facebook, 31 May.

Bush, D. (2012b), *The Flying Trapeze* (Bridgend: Seren).

Bush, D. (2014), 'Response to Minhinnick's submission to Greatest Welsh Novel', online (unavailable), Facebook, 1 October.

Bush, D. (2017), 'Primal Landscapes', *The Times Literary Supplement*, 24 March.

Bush, D. (2023), 'Robert Lowell', 'My Father's Tools', 'La France Éternelle', *Poetry Wales*, 59/1.

Bush, D., Curtis, T. and Jenkins, N. (1974), *Three Young Anglo-Welsh Poets* (Cardiff: Arts Council of Wales).

Unpublished sources

Duncan Bush, poems (provided by Annette Weaver, January 2021)

'Edwardian'
'Myths of the Fall'
'Neolithic'
'The Calais Caricatures'
'The Barn Owl'

Duncan Bush, prose (provided by Annette Weaver, January 2021)

'A Sense of Place'
'Interview at Atlantic College'
'Lavernock'
'Pond's Cold Cream'
'Praise'
'Relocate'
'Scrapbooks'
'Severn'
'Screen Life'
Untitled pieces

Other works consulted

Aaron, J. and Wynn Thomas, M. (2003), 'Pulling you through changes: Welsh writing before, between and after two referenda', in M. Wynn Thomas (ed.), *Guide to Welsh Literature*, vol. 7, *Welsh Writing in English* (Cardiff: University of Wales Press).

Abse, D. (1962), 'Return to Cardiff', *Poems, Golders Green* (London: Hutchinson).

Abse, D. (1977), 'Not Adlestrop', *Collected Poems, 1948–1976* (London: Hutchinson; Harmondsworth: Penguin Random House).

Adams, S. (1998), 'Mike Jenkins, Nigel Jenkins and Duncan Bush', in *PN Review*, 25/1 (September–October), 123.

Adams, S. (2023), *Letters from Wales: Memories and Encounters in Literature and Life* (Cardigan: Parthian), pp. 316–21.

Allen, G. (1973), 'Old Colliers', *Poetry Wales*, 9/3.

Anon. (2008), description of Allan Bush, *Last Bird Singing*, Seren Books website. Available at: *https://www.serenbooks.com/?s=last+bird+singing* Accessed September 2023.

Babel, N. (2002) (ed.), *The Complete Works of Isaac Babel* (New York: Norton).

Barnes, J. (2016), *The Noise of Time* (London: Jonathan Cape).

Briggs, M. and Jordan, P. (1954), *Economic History of England*, sixth edn, revised (London: University Tutorial Press).

Brigley, Z. and Evans, K. (2021) (eds), *100 Poems to Save the Earth* (Bridgend: Seren).

Brown, C. (n.d.), quoted on cover, D. Bush, *The Genre of Silence* (Bridgend: Seren, 1988).

Bush, A. (1986), 'In Memory of Benjamin Moloise (Hanged 17th October 1985)', in M. Elfyn and N. Jenkins (eds), *Poets Against Apartheid / Beirdd yn Erbyn Apartheid* (Cardiff: Wales Anti-Apartheid Movement).
Bush, A. (2008), *Last Bird Singing* (Bridgend: Seren).
Butler, S. (1985) (ed.), *Common Ground: Poets in a Welsh Landscape* (Bridgend: Seren).
Clark, P. (1997) (ed.) *Act One Wales: Thirteen One Act Plays* (Bridgend: Seren).
Constantine, P. (2002), in N. Babel (ed.), *The Complete Works of Isaac Babel* (New York: Norton).
Cope, P. (2021) *I Dig Margam* (Severn Publishing); online at *https://businesswales.gov.wales/walesruralnetwork*
Curtis, T. (1972), *The Deerslayers* (Neath: Cwm Nedd Press).
Curtis, T. (1974), *Album* (Swansea: Christopher Davies).
Dauncey, S. (1992), 'Review of *Glass Shot*, Duncan Bush', *Poetry Wales*, 28/1.
Dickey, J. (1970), *Deliverance* (Boston: Houghton Mifflin).
Eagleton, T. (1984), quoted on cover, D. Bush, *Aquarium* (Bridgend: Seren).
Elfyn, M. and Jenkins, N. (1986) (eds), *Poets Against Apartheid / Beirdd yn Erbyn Apartheid* (Cardiff: Wales Anti-Apartheid Movement).
Evans, P. C. and Bush, D. (2004–6) (eds), *The Amsterdam Review*, 1–3.
Finch, P. (1967–74) (ed.), *Second Aeon* (magazine).
Freidin, G. (2025), 'Isaac Babel', Encyclopaedia Britannica online. Available at: *https://www.britannica.com/biography/Isaac-Babel* Accessed September 2023.
Ginsberg, A. (1956), *Howl and Other Poems* (New York: City Lights Books).
Ginsberg, A. (1994), 'Notes for Howl and Other Poems', in P. Hoover (ed.), *Postmodern American Poetry: A Norton Anthology* (New York: W. W. Norton).
Goodreads website (2015, 2018), reviews of Duncan Bush, *Glass Shot*. Available at: *www.goodreads.com/book/show/6382909-glass-shot* Accessed 11 September 2015, 29 March 2018.
Gregson, I. (2005), 'Transplanted (Duncan) Bush', *Poetry Wales*, 41/1.
Jenkins, M. (1979), *Rat City* (Barry: Edge Press).
Jenkins, M. (1981), review of Duncan Bush, *Nostos*, *Poetry Wales*, 17/2.
Jenkins, N. (1979), *Circus* (Swansea: Swansea Poetry Workshop).
Jenkins, N. (1981), *Warhead* (Swansea: Megaton Press).
Jenkins, N. (1989), *John Tripp: Writers of Wales* (Cardiff: University of Wales Press).
Jenkins, N. (1998), *Ambush* (Llandysul: Gomer Press).

Jenkins, N. and Elfyn, M. (1987) (eds), *Glas-Nos: Poems for Peace / Cerddi dros Heddwch* (Machynlleth: CND Cymru).

Jones, D. (1937), *In Parenthesis* (London: Faber and Faber).

Jones, T. H. (1976), 'Back', in *Collected Poems* (Llandysul: Gwasg Gomer).

Katz, E. (1982), *International Film Encyclopedia* (New York: Papermac).

Knight, S. (2003), 'A New Enormous Music: Industrial Fiction in Wales', in M. Wynn Thomas (ed.), *Guide to Welsh Literature*, vol. 7, *Welsh Writing in English* (Cardiff: University of Wales Press).

La Prée, P. de – see Bush, D.

McCarthy, C. (1985), *Blood Meridian* (New York: Knopf).

McGill, J. – see Bush, D.

Mantel, H. (1993), quoted on cover of D. Bush, *Glass Shot* (Mandarin).

Mathias, R. (1978), 'Foreword', M. Stephens and P. Finch (eds), *Green Horse: An Anthology by Young Poets from Wales* (Swansea: Christopher Davies).

Mathias, R. (1986), *Anglo-Welsh Literature: An Illustrated History* (Bridgend: Seren).

Minhinnick, R. (1995) (ed.), *Green Agenda: Essays on the Environment of Wales* (Bridgend: Seren).

Minhinnick, R. (1997), 'A country that said "Yes"', editorial, *Poetry Wales*, 37/3.

Minhinnick, R. (2014), nomination of D. Bush, *The Genre of Silence*, for Greatest Welsh Novel, *Wales Arts Review*, 3/19.

Morson, G. S. (2002), 'Isaac Babel's Genre of Silence: A review of *The Complete Works of Isaac Babel*, edited by Nathalie Babel', *The New Criterion*, 20/5.

Ormond, J. (1991), 'Cathedral Builders', *Cathedral Builders and Other Poems* (Gregynog: Gwasg Gregynog).

Osbourne, A. (2020), 'A Help-sheet for Teachers: Notes on "Caroline: a county life"', Swansea University/Prifysgol Abertawe online. Available at: *https://www.swansea.ac.uk/media/BUSH-CAROLINE.pdf* Accessed September 2023.

Pagnoulle, C. (1995), 'Duncan Bush', Encyclopedia.com. Available at: *www.encyclopedia.com/arts/culture-magazines/bush-duncan* Accessed September 2023.

Poole, R. (1992a), 'Interview with Duncan Bush', *Poetry Wales*, 28/1.

Poole, R. (1992b), 'Duncan Bush's "personae"', *Poetry Wales*, 28/1.

Preston, A. (2016), 'The Noise of Time review – Julian Barnes's masterpiece', *Guardian*, 17 January. Available at: *https://www.theguardian.com/books/2016/jan/17/the-noise-of-time-julian-barnes-review-dmitri-shostakovich* Accessed September 2023.

Ramm, B. (2017), 'The writers who defied Soviet censors', BBC.com. Available at: *www.bbc.com/culture/article/20170724-the-writers-who-defied-soviet-censors* Accessed September 2023.
Richards, A. (1994), *The Penguin Book of Welsh Short Stories* (Harmondsworth: Penguin).
Saroyan, W. (1934), 'Seventy Thousand Assyrians', *Story*, April 1934.
Smith, D. (2008), Review of Allan Bush, *Last Bird Singing*, Seren Books website. Available at: *https://www.serenbooks.com/?s=last+bird+singing* Accessed September 2023.
Smith, D. (2014) (ed.), *Story: The Library of Wales Short Story Anthology* (2 vols) (Cardigan: Parthian).
Solzhenitsyn, A. (1968), *Cancer Ward* (London: The Bodley Head).
Sontag, S. (1979), *On Photography* (Harmondsworth: Penguin).
Stead, P. (1986), 'Wales in the movies', in T. Curtis (ed.), *Wales the Imagined Nation: Essays in Cultural and National Identity* (Bridgend: Seren).
Stead, P. (1991), *Richard Burton: So Much, So Little* (Bridgend: Seren).
Stephens, M. (1973), 'Ponies, Twynyrodyn', *Exiles All* (Triskel Poets 8).
Stephens, M. (1968), *Abber Jabber* (self-published).
Stephens, M. (2007), *Poetry 1900–2000* (Cardigan: Parthian).
Stephens, M. and Finch, P. (1978) (eds), *Green Horse: An Anthology by Young Poets from Wales* (Swansea: Christopher Davies).
Thomas, E. (1994), *Three Plays* (Bridgend: Seren).
Wales Online (2016), 'Why Cardiff will again be served by famous old "pick an orange" buses'. Available at: *https://www.walesonline.co.uk/news/wales-news/cardiff-again-served-famous-old-11282975* Accessed September 2023.
Webb, H. (1995), *Collected Poems* (Cardiff: University of Wales Press).
Williams, D. G. (2015), *Wales Unchained: Literature Politics and Identity in the American Century* (Cardiff: University of Wales Press).
Williams, N. (2002), 'Duncan Bush and the Parasitic Art', *Poetry Wales*, 38/2.
Wynn Thomas, M. (1999), *Corresponding Cultures: The Two Literatures of Wales* (Cardiff: University of Wales Press).

Personal correspondence

Phil Cope to Robert Minhinnick, 26 March 2023
P. C. Evans, two letters to Robert Minhinnick, 2022, 17 April 2023
Ian Gregson to Robert Minhinnick, 21 March 2023
Annette Weaver, three letters to Robert Minhinnick, May 2023, December 2023, 8 September 2024

Index